HELEN OF BURMA

Helen Rodriguez

COLLINS
8 Grafton Street, London W1
1983

William Collins Sons and Co. Ltd.
London · Glasgow · Sydney · Auckland
Toronto · Johannesburg

BRITISH LIBRARY CATALOGUING IN PUBLICATION DATA

Rodriguez, Helen
Helen of Burma.
1. World War, 1939–1945—Prisoners and persons,
Japanese
I. Title
940.54'72'520924   DB05.B1

. First published 1983
© Helen Preston 1983

ISBN 0 00 217002 7
Photoset in Sabon
by Rowland Phototypesetting Ltd
Bury St Edmunds, Suffolk
Made and printed in Great Britain by
William Collins Sons & Co. Ltd, Glasgow

Illustrations

Foreword

I met Helen Rodriguez only once, yet she left a mark on me that I will never forget. She was enormously fat, gross almost, but her presence was such that she gave an impression not of corpulence but of power and immense vitality. She was ugly by all the traditional standards of good looks, yet her courage and dignity lent her a kind of beauty. She was slowly recovering from a heart attack that had almost killed her, and it was the first time she had left her flat for several months. The soles of her feet had recently had to be lanced and the scars had become infected. Every time they touched the ground she was in agony. It took her eleven minutes to cover the thirty yards or so between the car and the restaurant table, shuffling a few inches at a time, her face grey with pain; joking, groaning, muttering to herself in ironical self-pity. Of course, we should have come to her in her home, but she had decided that it was time she went out and that was the end of it. When Helen made up her mind on what she ought to do, no mere mortal could deflect her.

Once she had reached her chair she took a few minutes to recover, but her brooding presence still dominated the table. When she began to talk she was at once the centre of attention: not because she talked long or loudly – she was, on the contrary, an excellent listener and by no means anxious to speak about herself – but because of the force of personality which came through in every word. Gradually she was coaxed into describing her life in Burma during the war; a matter-of-fact recital told with humour and a total absence of self-pity, of events so horrifying and pressures so relentless that it was hard to see how anyone could have withstood them. The Japanese could have killed Helen Rodriguez, almost did so many times, but nothing would have broken the spirit of the woman who was talking to us that night.

Some six months later the first draft of her memoirs arrived in Collins. Most of what she wrote was vouched for from other sources – the George Medal, for one thing, is not lightly given – yet her story might have seemed literally incredible if one had not known the author. It was a story of heroism so noble, dedication so absolute, endurance so determined, that one could only marvel at the infinite resources of mankind. No one could read *Helen of Burma* without feeling that the human race was the greater for having counted Helen Rodriguez among its number.

A little later she was dead, too early to see this book into its final form. Her over-taxed heart gave up, killing her as she slept. She would have enjoyed the reviews and articles, all the furore of publication; have disliked the personal publicity but have submitted to it with good grace and performed supremely well. As it is the book must stand as her monument; the story, simply and movingly told, of one of the great women of our generation.

Helen would not have wished this book to be published without paying a tribute to the work of her friend, Alfred Draper, whose advice and encouragement helped her enormously in the telling of her story.

PHILIP ZIEGLER

Chapter 1

—◆—

It was just after ten in the morning of 10th April that war descended on the peaceful hill station of Taunggyi. The silence was shattered by the scream of falling bombs, followed immediately by the crump of explosions, and the staccato chatter of machine guns. Within minutes the small capital of the Southern Shan States in upper Burma took on the appearance of a slaughter-house. The screams of the wounded and dying could be heard between the lulls, as the low-flying Japanese bombers and fighters peeled off and zoomed skyward in preparation for another attack. The bamboo and timber huts and houses collapsed into fragments and erupted in flames as if they had been doused in petrol. Anti-personnel bombs added to the carnage.

For hour after hour the Japanese pilots battered the defenceless town. It was an orgy of wanton destruction. For the highly skilled pilots it offered no greater hazards than a practice run; they were able to come in at ceiling-height, pick their targets and obliterate them at will. With total disregard for the rules of war, they paid special attention to the two hospitals: the British Military Hospital, housed in the old Shan Chiefs School, and the Civil Hospital of which I was matron at the relatively young age of twenty-six.

To those readers who only know hospitals through such imposing edifices as St Thomas's or St Bartholomew's, mine would have seemed a very modest affair. It was a single-storey building of brick and stone, with spacious verandas on every side and a sloping zinc roof that reverberated like a thousand kettle drums when the rains came. But to me it had everything: an out-patients department, a male surgical ward, an operating theatre, a women's ward which also housed the children, a dispensary and a male medical ward. My own quarters were two small but comfortable rooms in a modest staff block in the compound, which meant I did not have far to walk to and from work. It was also conveniently near my parents.

When the first stick of bombs fell, I was attending an elderly patient who had just had some toes amputated as a result of diabetes. As I washed him down, razor sharp slithers of glass cascaded around me as a stream of machine gun bullets shattered the windows. Knowing the poor man was incapable of movement, I grabbed hold of the mattress, pulled it on to the floor, and then lay on top of him. As the noise died away, I lifted my head and looked at the wall opposite. A neat row of bullet holes adorned the wall, looking as if they had been stitched there by some gigantic sewing machine. I realised that if I had not acted through instinct and dived for the floor, they would have ploughed through us both.

'Lie still, and stay there!' I shouted.

At the time it seemed a sensible thing to say, but I see now that my panic must have temporarily unhinged me, for I knew perfectly well that the poor fellow could not move an inch even if he wanted to.

The next few hours are a blur of unrelated but hideous incidents to which I can attach no chronological order. To me and my small staff, it seemed a holocaust. One minute we had been tending to the needs of those who were victims of nature's vast array of ailments, the next we were trying to cope with an assortment of man-made injuries that the devil himself could hardly have conjured up. Limbs were ripped off and already infected arms and legs shattered beyond recognition. Shrapnel and bullets left gaping, blood-pumping wounds; while a few were saved from witnessing the full horror around them – they were blinded.

When the planes eventually departed, their bomb bays

empty and ammunition expended, the Japanese began bombarding Taunggyi with heavy artillery.

It was a brutal and senseless mass slaughter, for the town was of little military importance; and the nearest railway was twenty-two miles away at Heho, and the road that linked Taunggyi to the railhead was so awful that the only way to travel it was by bullock cart. Yet the Japanese – deliberately one must suppose – chose to attack our town on bazaar day, when the market square was crowded with natives who had flocked in from nearby jungle villages to sell their fruit, vegetables, fish, woven goods and silver trinkets. It was a custom the Thaung Thu had followed for centuries.

I had known the Thaung Thu since my childhood, and no lovelier or more child-like people existed in Burma. They were as free as the air, with no guile or vices, and in a country where dacoitry abounded they did not know the meaning of murder or theft. The women who did the selling were as attractive in their features as the colourful traditional costumes they invariably donned for bazaar day: matching black tunics and skirts, with leggings and cuffs glistening and tinkling with the tiny silver rings they embroidered on them. The number of such charms was a rough-and-ready indication of their affluence; and, being a simple and somewhat superstitious people, the rings were also believed to contain magical protective qualities.

On their heads the Thaung Thu women wore six yards of bright red turban, and on their backs they carried their babies, papoose-fashion. They squatted on their haunches in front of the small piles of produce, as they had done since time immemorial, and waited for the first customers to arrive. The last thing they had imagined was that sudden death would strike from the skies as the fighters straffed them. Most of the women were struck across the chest as the planes zoomed low across the market square. It was a heartrending scene. Babies cried pitifully, the injured moaned in pain, and in the dust of the market place the crimson turbans lay in pools of blood. Bullocks which had been hit by shrapnel bellowed in pain. Most of the babies survived, for their mothers toppled backwards on top of them, protecting them from further attacks. Later, when many of these children ended up in my care, I could not help reflecting that death might have been a merciful release. Not only were they parentless, they were homeless as the Japs had completely destroyed the bamboo villages they lived in.

None of us had suspected that the Japanese were so close, nor would we have anticipated so cruel an assault even if we had been better informed. The onslaught caught the town completely unawares. Yet, looking back down the tunnel of the years, I think that I must have had some vague premonition of the impending disaster. It had always been my mother's habit to go to the bazaar, for little happened in Taunggyi and market day was the highspot of the week. For some unaccountable reason on this occasion, I had urged her not to go and she had bowed to my insistence. Even more remarkable, before going to the hospital that morning I had on the spur of the moment gone to the local post office and withdrawn my savings. To this day I do not know why I did so, except that I had a feeling they would be needed.

When the bombing and shelling finally ceased, a pitiful and seemingly endless procession of wounded and dying began to arrive at my hospital in bullock carts, prams and barrows – in fact, anything that would serve as transport. Some crawled in on shattered limbs, others were carried on the shoulders of those who had escaped unscathed. Suddenly my 120-bed hospital had more than four hundred patients.

The town was a scene of total devastation. Corpses, animal and human, littered the dusty streets, which were lined with the charred skeletons of burned-out houses and shops. There was an acrid smell of scorched flesh. People wandered around as if in a trance, trying to locate missing relatives and friends. The flies were already gathering in their millions. As I looked out of the hospital's shattered windows and saw the burning buildings topped by a pall of black smoke, I realised that the paradise I had known as Taunggyi had disappeared for ever.

*   *   *

But I have started in the middle of my story. Some explanation is needed as to how the eldest daughter of a Scottish mother and a Portuguese father came to be living in this Burmese Shangrila.

My father, Lambert Kenneth Rodriguez, had qualified as a doctor in India and had subsequently travelled to Edinburgh University for his FRCS (E). It was there that he met my mother, Mary, who was a nurse. Medicine ran in the family, for her father was professor of anatomy and physiology at the University. They fell in love and he asked permission to marry her; but in those days young Scottish girls of good upbringing were not permitted to marry dark-skinned strangers, even if they were Portuguese rather than anything more exotic. So my father returned home a bachelor. Two years later he was back in Edinburgh on a scholarship when he qualified for his MRCP, LRCP and DPH. He proved to be an outstanding doctor and his name still adorns the honours board at the University. He was as persistent in his courtship as he was in his medical studies, and he finally broke down the family resistance. An additional obstacle had been that he was a Roman Catholic and my mother a Protestant. In the end they decided to be married in both churches.

My father joined the Burma Medical Service and the newly-weds were posted to a remote station in the Chin Hills. I arrived on the scene on 24th October 1914. After war service in Mesopotamia and later Afghanistan, my father came back to Burma and held various positions in some of the less hospitable parts of the country – not that the Burmese were ever unfriendly but some of the other inhabitants could have been dispensed with; at one post my mother killed five snakes in the house in a single night. Then he was offered the job of civil surgeon in Taunggyi. As my mother's health was far from good my father suggested they should return to Scotland. She had never fully recovered from the 1919 flu epidemic in which our cook, syce and ayah had died. But when she set eyes on Taunggyi, Burmese for 'the big mountain', she knew that it was where she

[13]

wanted to live. 'It's so beautiful, it's just like home,' she said. And so they stayed.

Their home was the civil surgeon's house close to the hospital. It was a pleasant, comfortable building, but my father wanted a place he could call his own and not right on top of the job, so he set about building a rambling, mansion-style house on eight acres of land which he had purchased. It was an ambitious project, for the house would not have looked out of place in the heart of one of the more prosperous English counties. It took two years to build. My father hand-picked the carpenters and masons so as to ensure that all the work was of the finest quality, and he made sure that only the best materials were used. When it was completed he named it 'Craigmore' after my mother's home in Scotland. Then he lovingly landscaped the gardens, planted fruit trees and stocked the property with animals, geese and hens. A spacious paddock was set aside to house the horses and buffalo, and a large pond, almost a lake, was excavated. But my father was still not satisfied. When its owner moved to France, he bought Glenview, a bungalow which stood in four acres of land. There he grew a wide variety of crops and planted more trees, including extremely prolific walnuts. As the land stood below the reservoir he was able to utilise the overflow and construct an intricate irrigation system. The land was so fertile you only had to toss down a seed for it to sprout.

My mother enthusiastically furnished our two homes with heirlooms which had belonged to her parents and had laid in Thomas Cook's Rangoon warehouse for years as there had been no room in the government-furnished civil surgeon's house. The silver, crockery and Waterford glass were the envy of our neighbours; for most of the houses lived in by the British in Burma were furnished in a rather ornate oriental fashion, with goods made by local craftsmen. There was the odd piece of Chippendale among the furniture, but most of it was local and made of teak, since this wood was tough enough to withstand assault from ants and other such rapacious destroyers of sideboards and tables. The walls were adorned with paintings of Scottish landscapes, and with Persian carpets – too fine for the floors – which my father had bought at camel auctions in Afghanistan. The garden was a blaze of colour, with roses, honeysuckle and chrysanthemums in abundance. My mother became an orchid specialist and even managed to get some clumps of heather to take root.

It was an idyllic place in which to live. The climate was perfect, as we were 4,500 feet above sea level, and the views were spectacular; on clear days you could see the snows of China. I was entirely happy and asked nothing better than to be allowed to spend all my youth there. Unfortunately my parents felt that there was more to life than riding ponies in the hills, swimming in the so-clear water of Lake Imle (you could almost catch the fish with your bare hands), camping and running wild like a tom-boy, or taking a siesta on the back of the massively horned Mr White, my pet creamy-flanked buffalo. At the time I told them that they were being thoroughly unreasonable, and the dream of that paradise lost can still cause me pain, but even then I think I had a sneaking feeling that I must have some further education if I was to make anything worthwhile of my life.

And so my mother took me to Edinburgh and stayed there for a year while I was settling in. Then she left me with my grandmother and went back to join my father. I was happy enough, but I desperately missed my life in Taunggyi and counted the days till I could return. When my grandmother died, I realised the time had come. Without waiting to hear from my parents, I booked a passage from Liverpool, put myself in charge of the captain and sailed for home. I telegraphed my mother from Colombo asking her to meet me at the dockside in Rangoon. It was a wonderful homecoming, but also short-lived, for I was promptly packed off to Darjeeling to complete my schooling. Meanwhile my father retired and took up carpentry. As he jokingly liked to remark: 'Mr Sawbones became Mr Sawwood.'

[15]

When I returned to Taunggyi it was as if time had halted while I was away; nothing had altered. I remember Durbars where the European officers wore resplendent uniforms with swords at their sides and their women long, flowing summery dresses incongruously topped by bowler-hat shaped topis, and officials paraded in long swallow-tailed morning coats and stiff shirts. There were journeys across the lake in ornate barges propelled by the famous leg-rowers. I became a good shot, an expert angler, and adept at dressing up and making off with the top prizes at the numerous fancy dress balls. But pleasure could not continue unbridled. I had to start work some time.

It was, I suppose, only natural with my parents' background that I should decide on a career in nursing. I don't remember that I ever debated the matter very much; certainly I never went around telling people about my sense of vocation. I doubt if I even knew what a vocation was – in fact, I'm not even sure I know now! But, unlike the businessman who closes his office door and leaves his work behind him when he goes home, my parents' house had never been one in which 'shop' was a taboo subject. On the contrary, they talked constantly about their work and their responsibilities. As a sponge soaks up water, so I absorbed their evening talks about medicine and the privilege of healing. I unquestioningly accepted words like tradition, duty, service and devotion, without thinking that they were embarrassing clichés that had to be spoken of tongue-in-cheek, or better still not mentioned at all. I qualified, and worked for some time in Rangoon, until in August 1941 I was appointed matron of the Civil Hospital in Taunggyi.

At first I found my youth something of a problem. By tradition matrons are expected to have a severe demeanour and, like good timber, be seasoned by the years. I had very little in common with that image, so well known now since it has been projected by innumerable television soap operas about hospital life, nor did I look much like the equally traditional television nurse who wins the doctor's heart. My name might be Helen, but I had seen my face often enough in the mirror to know that it would never launch a thousand ships. My features were not unattractive, but they would never have graced the top of a chocolate box. In fact, they were quite suitable for my role in life. Over the years, too, I had acquired the ability to stamp my foot so as to attract attention and a voice that could command obedience without sounding too much of a martinet. I was fortunate in that I had inherited my father's bedside manner – a quality that cannot be learned from any books, which enabled me to convince people that the foul taste of medicine was a figment of the imagination, or that any little unpleasantness there might be was a small price to pay for the great good which they would be doing themselves by taking it. I also knew that a thermometer was the ideal weapon with which to silence a talkative or tiresome patient. Basically I was rather shy – my temperament could be described as introvert rather than extrovert – but a brusque attitude concealed my lack of self-confidence. Young though I might be, I still presented to the outside world quite a convincing picture of what I actually was – a matron of a government hospital in one of the most beautiful spots in the world.

* * *

Burma had remained untouched by the war. It was only real in Europe where Britain was fighting for its very existence. In Taunggyi life went on in its own leisurely, uninterrupted manner, for we had been constantly assured that Burma was a backwater of the Empire and no one would contemplate attacking it. And so the Europeans danced, drank and enjoyed themselves. It was not indifference, nor was it the recklessness of those who know their end is near. It was the same blindness to impending disaster which had made victims of the Titanic dance almost until the moment when the waves overwhelmed them.

The population of Taunggyi consisted of some one hundred and fifty Europeans, who included a handful of British officials and police, some Italian nuns, and a few missionaries. Because of its friendly climate a number of the better-off Burmese and Shan, Anglo-Indian and Anglo-Burmese lawyers, teachers and businessmen had also retired there. Few places on earth could have seemed more peaceful or unlikely to be touched by the horrors of global war. But we were living in a fool's paradise; ignoring the distant rumblings which gradually got closer and closer. I heard on my portable radio of the attack on Pearl Harbour which brought America into the war, of the invasion of Malaya and Thailand, and the sinking of the *Repulse* and *Prince of Wales* off the coast of Malaya. Still we stubbornly refused to face the facts. We knew we were at war, but we could not accept that we were in it.

On 23rd December, 1941, a massive force of Japanese bombers attacked the main port of Rangoon and almost brought it to a standstill. To be honest I don't remember the day for that reason; I recall it as the day my sister, Isabel, married Walter Fuller at the Church of the Sacred Heart in Taunggyi. It was a quiet wedding with only a handful of guests. The two matrons of honour, Walter's sisters Audrey and Fiona, had escaped the rape of Rangoon, for they were travelling up for the wedding. It was the last time I was to see them, for both died on the long trek to India, which began when the Japanese army swept through Burma. Their bodies, little more than skin and bone, were found by the roadside, clutching small scraps of paper on which was written the last will and testament of Mrs Wilby, the woman who had tried to lead them to safety. She had handed it to them shortly before she and three other children died.

The Governor of Burma, Sir Reginald Dorman-Smith, had exhorted everyone to stay at their posts: Burma, he announced grandly, was prepared for any onslaught. But after the first raid on Rangoon many people took his words for the bombast they were, and began to flock out of the city. The Japanese bombers hit Rangoon again on Christmas Day, and a further mass exodus began, with scores of thousands of people fleeing up-

[18]

country. Gradually Europeans and other refugees began arriving in Taunggyi. The breath of war was blowing down our necks, but still we did not heed it. The reports *must* be exaggerated. We had been led to believe that our forces were more than a match for these myopic little yellow men, while our fighters would shoot their obsolete planes from the skies. It was to be some time before we perceived the truth; that our soldiers were ill-equipped and untrained, and our air force was practically non-existent.

I was very scathing about the evacuation plans, which seemed to be a total shambles. For the life of me I could not understand why people were not being evacuated by sea from Rangoon, instead of being urged to go to the hills where few or no steps had been taken to receive them. Worse, how would they get away from Taunggyi if the need arose? Not that at that time I felt it conceivable that such a need *could* arise.

Life went on. There were cocktail parties, whist drives and dances at the Taunggyi Club, and I organised Red Cross classes for some of the wives, at which I taught them to make up wound-pads and pack medical boxes. Some visited the Shan Chiefs School, which had been turned into a temporary military hospital, to comfort the wounded soldiers who had fought so valiantly to stem the Japanese advance towards Rangoon.

I had little time for social life myself, as the hospital demanded most of my attention – there were always malaria and dysentery cases to treat, injuries and confinements to attend, appendices to remove, and hands to be held. The hospital was understaffed and overworked, and early on we had lost our surgeon, Colonel Ted Kingston, who was called into the army. He was replaced by an elderly, near-senile Sino-Burman surgeon who, poor man, should have been left in happy retirement. In addition, there were six Shan nurses, who had been trained by that amazing American missionary-doctor Gordon Seagrave, four ward servants, and the same number of native doctors.

Our task wasn't made any easier by the sudden influx of

refugees, some of whom installed themselves in our private rooms. A few of the white women arrived with jewellery and valuable coins sewn into the hems of their clothes. For some reason this angered me. Looking back, I feel I was being over-critical, what on earth was wrong with making sure you had the means of purchasing survival? But at the time it seemed to me to smack of self-preservation at the expense of everything else. All I can say to excuse myself is that I have a tinder-box temper: the legacy, my father thought, of the 1919 Spanish flu epidemic which had so nearly killed me.

I must confess that Burma's memsahibs did irritate me beyond measure; not all of them, of course, but those among them whose idea of 'service' was that it was something one did on a tennis court. It was not a question of my not suffering fools gladly, for they were anything but foolish; on the contrary many were highly intelligent and well educated. I see now that they were the victims of a system. They were not to blame for their attitude, for the rigid class structure encouraged them to be idle. Once they had married a Burra sahib they did not need to know what it was to make a bed or cook a meal. They were surrounded by native servants who relieved them of all menial household chores, even to the extent of looking after their children. They were encouraged in their indolence by husbands who did not believe in keeping a dog and barking themselves. Self-reliance was not encouraged. When the chips were down during the historic trek to India, many revealed great inner strength and the stuff that heroines are made of, but little of that hidden quality was evident when they arrived in Taunggyi. The Club became the hub of their existence; there they could pursue all those activities that kept the memsahib superior, remote, and aloof from the many-strataed population which did not have white skins.

Today people go out of their way to acquire an out-of-season tan, but in those times, in a land where the sun shone brilliantly, women sought the shade to nurture and protect an ivory skin, for pallor was a visible sign of class. If I did not share their passion for sun-shades and long gloves, it was not because my parentage excluded me from joining their exclusive community – I was never ostracised on the grounds of colour for the simple reason that both my parents were European – but because the fetish of whiteness was alien to everything in which I had been brought up to believe.

My complexion was what a romantic novelist might describe as honey-coloured. If I had been an Anglo-Burmese or Anglo-Indian in Taunggyi, I would have had to suffer taunts such as 'café au lait', 'one of coffee, two of milk', or the most scornful and offensive of all, 'a touch of the tar brush'. As I was half-Scots and half-Portuguese I was spared such attentions.

I had no idealistic wish to change my lot, no objection to sharing my nationality with Vasco da Gama and Robert Burns, not to mention my beloved parents. But this did not mean I felt superior to other races. On the contrary, I was intolerant of women who would walk off a dance floor because they saw an eligible European bachelor dancing with a pretty girl whose skin wasn't of the purest Dresden china. I was not, let me hasten to say, a forerunner of today's militant anti-racists. I am no crusader. I can't recall ever standing on a soap box bemoaning the fate of the less fortunate, or demanding an end to the monstrous inequality of our social system. But I would have applauded those who did. Experience had taught me the unimportance of race divisions, and it was not a lesson I was ever to forget.

Nursing is a down-to-earth profession and there is no greater social leveller than the bed pan. One quickly learns that skin pigmentation doesn't matter a damn; all blood is red beneath the skin, or to be more accurate, if it is 'blue', then you are probably on the way to the graveyard. Suffering pays no attention to accent or colour. But even if my work had not pushed me in that direction, I would have felt the same since I had been brought up in a devout, if not overwhelmingly religious household, where we were encouraged to believe that heaven was a multi-racial community. I imagined it like a larger, grander version of the old classroom picture showing Victoria, the Queen Empress, surrounded by the dusky-skinned children from her family of nations.

We had our servants, of course, but my father insisted that even if we did not treat them as total equals, we should always remember they were humans. We were forbidden to speak to them in English – as a result I spoke fluent Urdu, Burmese and Hindustani – and they had their own plot of land on which they grew and reared exactly the same crops as we did. Burma was my birthplace, and though I knew I was not Burmese, I did not align myself with those who talked nostalgically of 'Home' and tried to reproduce the habits and customs of England on an alien soil.

Like that heavenly poet but feet-on-the-ground priest, John Donne, I did not want to be aloof, but a part of the continent, a piece of the main. I did not want my life to centre around an island – 'The Club' – which was treated as reverently by the worshippers as though it stood on a sacred plot that had been shipped out from Surrey.

The Club was the bastion of white supremacy, as vital to the European way of life as the pagoda was to the Burmese. Even though the enemy was steadily moving northwards, leaving behind a wake of unspeakable atrocities, the Club remained inflexibly British and obstinately unruffled. Immaculately-clad stewards padded silently across the well-furnished, plush-carpeted lounge, dispensing 'burra pegs' and 'chota pegs' of whisky, gin and brandy. There was a smoke-room and billiard room for the men, a bridge room for the ladies, an excellent restaurant and snack bar, a swimming pool, and carefully tended tennis courts. It was also the centre for interminable gossip, rumour and backbiting. I had never given it a great deal of thought until it became a luxurious transit camp for refugees. If I dwell on it now, it is because one has to understand it in order to appreciate the atmosphere prevailing at the time, and the reason for Burma being caught with its pants down. The leisurely life style which the Club symbolized added fuel to the

Japanese claims that the Burmese were an exploited people who would be helped by the invaders to shed the yoke of imperialism. In a way it was the rule of the Club from which the Burmese were anxious to be liberated. As a result, a strong and active fifth column emerged, and many of the refugees of all races, classes and religions were to die at its hands during the epic trek to India.

Meantime the chronicle of disasters continued unabated, but we lived on in blissful ignorance. We had no newspapers and the little we picked up on the radio was soothing and optimistic. Those in authority feared that the truth would undermine morale. Refugees did begin to fly out or to head to Lashio, but most of them hung on. The Japanese would never come – Sir Reginald Dorman-Smith himself had said so.

Even when Rangoon was abandoned to the enemy in early March, there were still many who refused to face the obvious. They resembled an inept doctor who could not diagnose a disease until it was proved terminal. It was not to be very long before the need for diagnosis no longer existed. On the morning of 10th April the truth became brutally apparent.

The day before, an old friend, Colonel Kingston, had turned up unexpectedly in Taunggyi to buy some of the huge fish which were plentiful in the lake. He was a cool, calm man, not given to panic, and so I heeded his words with especial care. 'They are starving in Meiktila,' he explained. 'The Japs are getting very close now. Get your mother and father out while there is still time.'

As a result of his warning I pleaded with my father to leave for India with my mother while aircraft were still flying out. He refused. My father was considerably older than my mother, though the disparity in their ages did not really emerge until they had been married for many years. Probably his age coupled with his ill health had a lot to do with his reluctance to leave. He may have believed he would be a hindrance on the arduous struggle that would have to be faced before getting to an airfield, or boarding a plane. He may just have felt deep

[23]

reluctance to leave his home, where he was surrounded by all the mementos of a happy and fulfilled life. Whatever the reason, he stubbornly insisted that he would stay where he was. There was no time for further pleas before the Japanese aeroplanes were upon us.

My recollection of events on that first day is extremely hazy; so much happened that there was never time to pause and take stock of the situation. As the first wave of planes passed on after attacking the hospital, I saw the old surgeon walking aimlessly around a shattered ward, picking up pieces of glass and putting them in his pocket. I realised he had lost his reason; whether through shock or blast did not really seem to matter. He was clearly of no further use in the hospital, more a hindrance in fact, and the most humane thing to do was to encourage him to leave. There were too many people in desperate need of medical attention to waste time or tears over an old man who had slipped into a twilight world of unreality. In some ways, perhaps, he was the luckiest person in the ward. The rest of us had wounds to dress, gaping holes to stitch up, the uninjured to transport to the slit trenches, babies to feed and the dead to move out of sight. The bodies soon overflowed our tiny mortuary, which had been built to cater for death on a less catastrophic scale.

In the middle of all the chaos and bustling confusion, one of the ward cleaners came up to me and tugged urgently at my skirt. 'Memsahib, come quick. Bomb making noise,' she muttered and she pursed her lips and made a hissing sound.

I hurried out to the compound and to my dismay saw a huge bomb nestling in a room-sized crater not far from the operating theatre. To this day I would swear that it was making a hissing noise, though I have since been assured that this must have been a product of my imagination, or more likely ringing in the ears caused by the incessant din of the bombing. I hastily scribbled a note on a scrap of paper and gave it to a native ward servant with instructions to take it to Jock Garratty, the garrison engineer. If he did not come up immediately and do something about the bomb, I told him, there would be no hospital left for him to visit.

I stood gazing at the missile as if hypnotised, expecting it to erupt at any second. Then I shrugged and turned away; Taunggyi was already being battered beyond recognition by high explosives, one more bomb would not make a lot of difference. I went back to the patients and worked automatically, for however consoling my reasoning might be, it signally failed to distract my mind from the bomb and the man who had been despatched with the message. After what seemed an eternity he returned, to announce breathlessly that Jock was away on urgent business and could not be contacted. I had visions of the death roll mounting before he could spare the time to visit us, and attend to the bomb.

It was then that I remembered the magazine I had seen lying on the table at my parents' home. My father had been a regular subscriber to *Scientific American*, and a recent edition had displayed a cross-section drawing of a bomb with instructions on how to defuse it. I recalled thinking at the time what a waste of time and space such articles were, but it was typical of the patriotic wartime fever, that led editors to think it their duty to make their readers feel as if they were in the front line. I do not imagine that it ever occurred to the author that anyone would have to rely on his article to tackle such an emergency in real life. I sent my messenger off again to fetch the magazine and retreated with it to a quiet corner.

Apart from changing a punctured tyre or an oxygen cylinder, my mechanical knowledge was minimal, and so I pored over the drawing until every detail was indelibly printed on my mind. The article made the mechanism of a bomb sound relatively simple and in half an hour or so I had learned where everything vital was located. Then I went down to the generating plant, where we kept our supply of tools, and helped myself to a whole lot of spanners, wrenches and screwdrivers. I thought to myself as I walked slowly up to the crater: 'You'd better not tell anyone about this.' As I clambered down into the hole and crouched alongside the bomb, I looked up and saw the elderly Gurkha servant gazing down at me. 'You will blow the place to pieces,' he said matter-of-factly. I did not need his comment, for the thought had only too clearly occurred to me too. Irritably I shouted up: 'Just you don't open your mouth to anyone.' He did not, but very wisely he evacuated the women and children, who were too close for comfort, to a nearby school.

The sweat was pouring down my face, my uniform clinging to me as if I had been drenched with a hose, and my hand shaking uncontrollably as I attached a spanner to the side of the bomb. Gingerly I attempted to unscrew what the diagram assured me was the fuse. The spanner was rattling so loudly against the casing that I felt sure the vibration would set off the bomb. At least whatever it was I was unscrewing came out quite easily. When I had done all that the article had described, I clambered out and went back into the wards. I was even deaf to the cries of the injured, for my ears were waiting for the enormous explosion I was certain was bound to come. Two hours must have passed before Jock Garratty turned up and said: 'I hear you've got an unexploded bomb, Helen. Let's go and have a look at it.'

I turned to him and, feeling extremely foolish, said, 'I've had a go at defusing it, Jock.'

He simply nodded and walked towards the crater, surveyed it, then clambered down. When he got out his face was split in an ear-to-ear grin. 'You know something, Helen, it's perfectly harmless.' I wasn't quite sure what he meant, and I was darned sure I wasn't going to ask him to elaborate. Maybe, by good luck and God's guidance, I had defused it, but I had ruined my nerves in the process, and the last thing I wanted to know was that my efforts had been needless. As far as I'm concerned I had passed out with flying colours as a bomb disposal expert. Anyway, the bomb stayed in its crater like a slumbering monster, and it never came out of hibernation.

There was little of Taunggyi left standing at the end of the day. Main Street, which had been lined with Indian shops where we purchased our drink, corned beef, biscuits and tea, was a row of charred and smouldering shells. The Cycle Mart, which had sold everything from sweets and shoes to torches and batteries, no longer existed. The tiny cinema would never show another film. Corpses still lay in grotesque postures, for they were beyond help, and the rescue parties had sensibly concentrated on those who could be saved.

Panic had set in among the civilian population, and a mass migration began towards Lashio and places offering an illusion of safety. Refugees who had arrived laden-down with all their worldly goods, abandoned everything that might impede their escape. I was suddenly swamped with unwanted pets: dogs, cats, parrots and even geese.

I realised that I could no longer delay getting my mother to safety. My father had already made up his mind that he would stay behind in his beloved Taunggyi and even if I had thought him wrong I knew I would never be able to persuade him to change his mind. There was no point in my mother staying behind so as to keep him company, for even if they were together when the Japanese captured them, there was little chance that they would be imprisoned in the same compound. She was white, and although he was a European, his complexion was dark.

That night the native doctors shamefacedly handed me their keys and announced that they were leaving. I did not blame them in the least, for any Burmese who stayed at their posts would be considered traitors by the "liberators" and might well face execution. I also knew that if my four Shan nurses remained behind they might well be raped and slaughtered by the enemy. Apart from that, I could scarcely ask them to remain, or remind them of their duty, for no one in authority had made any plans to help them evacuate in an emergency, and they could be forgiven for thinking that, as they were coloured, they had been left to fend for themselves. Quite enough Europeans in posi-

[27]

tions of responsibility had already fled, to give them good grounds for their belief.

Taunggyi, at the time of the attack, could only boast three motor cars. One of these, an old Dodge saloon which belonged to my father, performed a multitude of tasks from ambulance to local taxi service for out-patients. I had anticipated using it as a getaway car when the moment came, but it was promptly commandeered by an army officer, who used it to head for Lashio, well loaded with his personal belongings. Somehow or other I had to get hold of transport if my mother and those of the patients who were fit enough to travel were to escape.

Time was running desperately short, for although there was little left standing in the town I was in no doubt that the planes would be back. I despatched search parties round the derelict town, and somebody managed to find the remains of an old lorry. It looked totally derelict, but fortunately one of the doctors, who had an uncanny skill with engines, got it running. I sent out more search parties and they came back with an assortment of tyres, a battery, and most important, some cans of petrol. The floor of the lorry was covered with mattresses, and the more serious cases and those in need of emergency operations were placed on top. Then the nurses and doctors squeezed in where and how they could. I said to the driver: 'Get them to Lashio and to my sister.' My mother, who was under the impression that I was going to join them, kept calling out: 'Please come, Helen, please get in.' I told her I would follow as soon as father was fit to travel, but I knew that he would never budge from Craigmore.

I stood in the road, a figure of utter dejection, and watched the overloaded lorry, sagging on its springs, bump jerkily along the road with its pathetic cargo of human flotsam. My mother was weeping and waving. It was the last I saw of her for three and a half years.

I walked slowly back to the hospital and the remaining patients. Waiting at the entrance to welcome me was Ma Sein, or Annie as I called her, my Shan servant. Her white Burmese

[28]

jacket was bloodstained and her *loongyi* (skirt), usually so spotless and immaculate, was covered with filth. She and I were now in sole charge of the remaining sick and wounded. I was sorely tempted to turn around and take the road for Lashio, but through the blasted windows I suddenly caught the sound of people in agony.

And of course the Japs did return, again, and again, and again.

Annie and I worked like sleep walkers in a trance. We tended the wounded as best we could, but more and more continued to arrive. I realised that I would have to preserve carefully my small hoard of medicine and drugs, and morphine was only administered to those who could no longer bear the pain. Normal hospital cleanliness and routine had to be abandoned, and we could only keep the wards clean of blood and reasonably hygienic by washing them out with the fire hoses.

I was told that a convoy of lorries would soon be arriving to evacuate the sick, and that I was to accompany them, but they failed to turn up and all we could do was wait, hope and pray. The plight of the patients kept me too busy to worry about my own safety.

As a precaution I collected as much of the stores as I could and distributed them in small consignments around the hospital, so that they would not fall into the hands of looters. My strategy proved a waste of time, for marauders rooted out most of the caches and made off into the jungle. The surgical instruments I packed into a huge basket, which I never let out of my sight.

When you are dog-tired and falling alseep on your feet you begin to act like an automaton, and habit dictates your movements, so that you perform tasks quite unaware of what you are doing. Without Annie I could never have managed, indeed her efforts were more praiseworthy than mine for she had the added anxiety of not knowing where her husband and small son might be. Together we cleared away the night soil, that pleasant euphemism for human excreta, boiled all the water, buried the dead, and did everything we could to prevent outbreaks of disease, a very real risk in view of the rough and ready measures we had to adopt.

Day and night ceased to have any meaning in the blacked-out wards. It was just twenty-four hours of non-stop drudgery, and the smooth running of the hospital assumed a very makeshift aspect. If I had not been the matron myself, I might often have asked apprehensively what matron would say when she saw what was going on. I had no time for paper work, and only kept the minimum of records necessary to follow the progress of the patient. Certainly there was no time for the detailed day and night log I had insisted on the nurses keeping in happier days. I snatched the odd hour's sleep whenever I could, but it was never enough and I was perpetually on the brink of crippling exhaustion.

For a long time afterwards I had only a very blurred memory of what I did. I suppose it should have been the proudest moment in my career yet the picture had somehow faded. People sometimes accused me of false modesty when they asked me to tell them about this period. Modesty had nothing to do with it; I think that probably I was reluctant to talk about it because I had no wish to revive memories of such an unhappy time. Subconsciously I must have blotted out the details. They were too painful to recall. It is only with the passing of the years that I have been able to look back dispassionately and, as details come flooding back, complete the picture, as one gradually pieces together a jig-saw puzzle. Even after so many years I am still moved to tears.

During one attack the improvised Military Hospital became the main target for a fierce enemy bombardment. The surrounding hills echoed to the thunder of unseen guns, and I could hear the screech of the shells as they headed for the hospital a mile or so from my own. Then a stranger burst into the ward and said: 'Please come quickly. There are sick soldiers there.' I had been too busy with my own problems over the last few days to pay a visit to the Military Hospital, or for that matter to give it any attention. If I thought about it at all, it was to assume that it had been evacuated. Now my unexpected caller disappeared. I knew I would have to go and see for myself what was going on and what could be done for the inmates.

I ran to the hospital, which was near the Durbar Hall, not knowing what I would encounter. Shells were falling quite close to the building as I approached the main entrance, and from what I could see it seemed deserted. Then when I went inside I heard the sound of men calling for help. I hastened towards the cries and found a number of badly wounded sepoys and some Chinese soldiers, crouched in terror on their beds. They were in a bad way with fractured arms and legs, spinal injuries and bullet and splinter wounds. One enormous soldier was so depressed at being abandoned that he was crying uncontrollably. An Indian soldier, who spoke perfect English, said plaintively: 'We have not eaten for two days.' I scurried through the building yelling out for stretcher bearers, but all I heard was the echo of my own fear-laden voice. I realised that unless something was done, and quickly, the handful of men would die in their beds, for the Japanese gunnery was remarkably accurate: the building was slowly disintegrating before my eyes.

I was, by present day pin-up standards, what would be described euphemistically as a well-built young woman, but I had not eaten properly for days and I was feeling extremely weak in the legs. I had therefore very little idea what I was hoping to achieve when I said: 'Don't worry. I'll try and get you out of here. You must do all you can to help me, though.' I hope I sounded more confident than I felt. I cannot imagine what help I supposed they would be able to give me, for several of them were so badly wounded that they were incapable of movement. There was a giant of a Pathan, well over six feet tall and weighing at least twelve stone, who looked at me and asked, 'How can you help? We are too big.' I told him not to worry, somehow or other I would cope.

I decided that the sensible course would be to get the most

seriously injured out first, and that as the Pathan was one of them I might as well start with him. I sat on the edge of his bed and urged him to try to cling to my back. He made a super-human effort to get his arms around my shoulders, and after an eternity of puffing and panting I managed to rise to my feet and hoist him fireman-fashion over my shoulder. I staggered out of the building like a drunken coalman, and succeeded in getting him to the comparative safety of a slit trench before going back for another soldier. I wondered how long it would be before the hospital was totally destroyed, for the Japanese showed no sign of switching their target. I knew that when the time came to carry the injured back to my own hospital it would be physi-cally impossible for me to carry more than one at a time. I would only be able to hope that the others would survive while I was away. I knew that I could not call for any assistance as there wasn't a soul in sight.

I lost count of the number of times I carried men from their beds to the slit trench – eight, ten, a dozen. Then I hoisted the burly Pathan on to my back and began to stagger towards my hospital by way of a short cut past the Durbar Hall and through the Treasury Compound. The soldier was so heavy that I had to make frequent halts to get my breath back and regain my strength. My main fear was that once I had put him down I would not be able to hoist him up again. It was here that Taunggyi's monsoon drainage system came to my aid. During the wet season the rainfall is so heavy that enormous sewer-sized pipes had been erected alongside the roads to carry away the sudden deluge. We called them culverts, for they were encased in a thick layer of protective concrete which raised them some three feet above the surface of the road. I was able to lower the Pathan on to this throne while I took a brief rest, and there was no great problem in getting him back on my shoulders again.

By the time I reached my hospital I was totally exhausted, but I was determined to make one more trip before stopping for the day. I had to take some food up to the near-starving men, and anyway wanted to bring one more of the soldiers to comparative safety.

After distributing the food to the soldiers who were still in the hospital, I assured them that I would be back first thing in the morning. Then I went out to the slit trench, hoisted another soldier on to my back and began the arduous journey home. By now there was a distinct slackening of the barrage, and I consoled myself with the thought that when nightfall came it would cease altogether. It did in fact, but it was renewed with added intensity when I set off at first light next morning with more food, and the firm intention of removing everyone who was left in the hospital to the slit trenches.

I had only travelled a short distance with a wounded soldier on my back when I felt a violent blow on the leg which sent me crashing to the ground. My calf was sticky with blood where I had been hit by a piece of shrapnel or a stray bullet. Amazingly, perhaps due to my exhausted condition, I did not experience any great pain, and I was able to pick up the sepoy and get him into the trench. After treating my wound as best I could and staunching the flow of blood, I continued emptying the ward. Then help arrived from a most unexpected quarter, in the form of a Chinese patient who was suffering from tuberculosis. Having learned of my plight he had insisted on leaving his bed in the Civil Hospital to give me some support, although he was in far worse shape than I was. When we had at last got everyone to the slit trenches, we cowered against the sides until there was a lull in the shelling.

It was only then that I realised that we had accomplished the easy part of our task; the tough part still lay ahead. Somehow or other we had to get the wounded men back to my own hospital; no mean task for a wounded woman and a sick old man.

I scoured the neighbourhood for a bullock cart, but it seemed that every animal in the area had either fled into the jungle or been purloined by refugees. There was nothing to do but carry them down. The coughing and spitting Chinaman helped to hoist the soldiers on to my back and tie them securely in position with a blanket. Then together we began the seemingly endless journey down to the hospital.

After three or four trips my leg was giving me hell, but I could not bring myself to groan, much as I felt like it, for the soldiers who were so badly wounded went through their ordeal without even a whimper. In fact they encouraged me to keep going by muttering: 'Nearly there. Nearly there.' During each trip we made good use of the monsoon culverts; without them we could never have managed. Even as it was, I several times almost dropped my burden and was on the threshold of total exhaustion by the time I reached my hospital.

When I had safely deposited half a dozen wounded men in beds, I got Annie to help me put a fresh dressing on my leg before setting out again with the elderly Chinese. Annie also insisted on coming. I told her that someone had to remain behind to look after the sick, and that only she possessed the necessary knowledge, but she was adamant. What is more, she proved extremely inventive by suggesting we build a make-shift *dhoolie:* a kind of sedan chair in which European women and their children were carried to the hill stations during the hot weather. I rummaged around my quarters until I found a cane chair to which we lashed long bamboo poles, rather like the shafts in a horse-drawn cart. It looked extremely fragile and precarious, but it proved to be effective. As I hobbled off between the front shafts, I could not help recalling that when I first applied to be a nurse, the interviewer had expressed doubts about my physical fitness – I was too delicate, he said.

It took us four days to clear the Military Hospital. Three and a half years later I learned that I had been awarded the George Medal, for 'the utmost courage and devotion to duty'. The medal is my most prized possession, but if the clock could be turned back, I would willingly have foregone the honour for just one old wooden-wheeled bullock cart.

Chapter 2

The Japanese bombers now gave Taunggyi a temporary respite, and Annie and I were able to begin restoring some semblance of order in the hospital. I don't think it was out of compassion that they left us alone; just that there was so little left for them to demolish. Taunggyi was by now little more than a ghost town. A number of British administrators and their staff still remained at their posts, but there was little for them to administer, and one morning the Commissioner, Freddie Pierce, called on me and said the time had come for me to think about leaving, and to draw up a list of evacuees. This I did, but I explained that I could not go myself as some of my patients were too sick to move, and I couldn't possibly desert them. On top of that there was my father living alone in Craigmore with a handful of loyal servants who refused to leave him.

I mumbled something about my duty and staying at my post as the Governor had urged. Freddie was a patient and kind man whom I had known since childhood. He must have thought I was a silly and pig-headed girl but he kept his views to himself and argued that I need not feel any remorse if I left now as I had done all that was humanly possible. I'm afraid I answered rather sharply and told him to look after his officials and I would look after my patients. I was not over-impressed at the way some of the civil servants had put the safety of their own skins before their responsibilities, and got out while the going was good, and my resentment made me less tolerant of Freddie's well-meaning proposals than I should have been.

Again I was promised some trucks, but again the promised transport failed to materialise. I did not blame anyone for this.

Burma was in a state of complete chaos by then, and the promises were made in good faith. Owing to the scorched earth policy adopted by the retreating British forces, to prevent anything of military value falling into enemy hands, there was an acute shortage of all kinds of transport, and an orderly fighting retreat was further hampered by the tens of thousands of refugees who choked the roads leading to India. They were dying by the roadside in their hundreds from cholera, dysentery, malaria, wounds and starvation. On top of that, dacoits and fifth columnists were murdering a great many. What was my handful of patients against such a mammoth problem? The jungles and roadsides were littered with the mounds of unmarked graves. At least those who died in my hospital had the benefit of a decent, if crude, burial with a hastily offered prayer.

By now my list of patients had been considerably reduced but there was still more work than Annie and I could cope with. But I had made my decision, and if I had prepared myself a bed of nails I had no one to blame but myself.

The next day Colonel Brocklehurst, who commanded Special Service Detachment 2 – a commando unit which had been trained at the secret Bush Warfare School under 'Mad Mike Calvert' and which specialised in the demolition of bridges – turned up at the hospital and warned me that they had been detailed to carry out an extensive programme of bridge-blowing as the Japs were quite close. Their task was to delay the advance and thus give the retreating army with its attendant mass of refugees as long a period of grace as possible. They had been operating quite near Taunggyi and had witnessed the horror of the first Japanese attacks. The colonel, a tall, raw-boned man with a huge revolver strapped to his side, resembled a fictional hero from some schoolboy's adventure book. He spoke quietly with a well-bred, well-educated voice, but his tones could not disguise the tungsten strength beneath the almost nonchalant exterior. He was, I learned later, a nephew of Queen Mary, and had been big game hunting with the Duke of Windsor when he was Prince of Wales. He had fought with Wingate in Abyssinia, and had a distinguished war record in the Middle East.

He explained that time was running out for the handful of 'last ditchers' who still remained in the town. Soon the fuse would reach the powder keg. When his men had completed their demolition they would pull out, and he expected me to be with them. He made it sound more like an order than a request, and he was clearly a man who expected to be obeyed. I replied that, as we still had a little time, I would continue to attend to my patients, and would reconsider the situation when things got more difficult. I could not bring myself to go through the Casablanca bit again – whether he thought me a heroine or a tiresome nuisance there would inevitably be arguments, and I had no energy to spare for such a diversion.

Colonel Brocklehurst nodded curtly, as if he had no great objection to my ideas, and then added that, when and if their duties permitted, he would allocate me six men to assist in running the hospital. He was as good as his word, for the six, including a sergeant, arrived the same day to say they had orders to help in whatever way they could, and that any instructions I issued would be obeyed.

They were all battle-hardened men who, rather belatedly, had been taught to emulate the Japs and to live off the jungle. The sergeant was an old sweat who hid a marshmallow heart under a tough exterior, and he had the irrepressible humour of the London East-Ender who could always see a bright side to things no matter how dark the situation seemed.

They brought their own food, awful cement-hard biscuits and bully beef, stubbornly refusing to diminish our store of rations. But I insisted they should have the occasional chicken or duck, which refugees had dumped on me and which I had cussed over at the time, never thinking they would so soon prevent us from starving.

John, the sergeant, made it abundantly clear to the men that when I gave an order it was as good as if it came from his own parade ground. What's more, he told me that when it came to following medical instructions, the three white stripes on his khaki tunic didn't count for a thing. They had all volunteered for the hazardous tasks they were undertaking without asking what was entailed; and this was as true of their new duties as of blowing bridges. So if it meant forming up the bed-pan brigade, or cleaning out the primitive toilets, the answer was: 'We shouldn't have volunteered.'

I split the lads – they were no more than that – into three groups, and gave them six-hour shifts, so that the hospital was constantly manned twenty-four hours a day. The bombing, straffing and bombarding began again, as if the enemy was determined to remove all trace of Taunggyi from the face of Burma. They were then only twelve miles away in Hopong, and advance parties established artillery batteries on a crag over-looking the town and subjected what remained of it to a non-stop barrage. The first salvoes were accompanied by the cacophonous din of kerosene tins being banged with sticks, the only means the remaining natives had of sounding the alarm. Soon the guns were joined by heavy mortars and machine gun fire. The wounded continued to arrive. I was amazed at the way in which the soldiers tackled their gruesome tasks. They were as gentle and conscientious as trained medical orderlies. They even cleared the place of broken glass and debris, and set to work to make the dispensary look something like it had in the old days. They scoured the littered floor, like misers looking for a lost halfpence, and recovered pills from shattered bottles, bandages, lint and much needed drugs like quinine. They appreciated that every find, no matter how small, could result in a life saved.

The hospital suffered several direct hits, and even more damage was caused by the blast from nearby explosions. As much of the building was made out of timber, fires quickly started. We had to evacuate one entire ward as there was a grave danger of the patients being burned alive. We were so short of space that mattresses were laid out on the veranda, and we even put up makeshift beds in the store rooms and kitchen.

I never heard a word of complaint from the soldiers; no task was too menial for them, and none too demanding. They evacuated those capable of being moved into the slit trenches during particularly heavy raids, then rushed off to fight fires, at the same time keeping a sharp eye open for marauders who were pillaging and looting anything within sight. On top of that they acted as stretcher bearers for the freshly wounded. Although every drop of water was carefully boiled, I knew we could not continue to ward off the scourges of cholera and dysentery, for some of the patients who had crawled in for help had been living in the most appalling conditions imaginable. Inevitably they brought disease with them.

Dead continued to pile up in the mortuary as we waited in vain for relatives to claim the bodies. The tough soldiers, who had up till now shown great respect for the dead, began to display a callousness born of harsh reality. Like me they realised that if the dead remained unburied they would merely increase the toll, as the corpses lay for hours draped with dried sisal leaves and crawling with flies, the stench of decay heavy in the air. At first we managed to keep the sickening odour in check by the liberal use of disinfectant, but that was becoming extremely scarce and was needed for more important things than keeping the dead sweet-smelling. Many were buried in the slit trenches which had been dug as air raid shelters, but everyone was kept so busy there wasn't time for formal burial parties. In any case, there were always fresh corpses to replace the old ones.

In time it became obvious that burial was no safeguard against the risk of an epidemic. The only entirely safe way to eliminate the danger would be by cremation. I pressed for this but Colonel Brocklehurst, normally so helpful and anxious to go out of his way to meet my requests, was hesitant. 'I daren't risk that,' he said. 'A bonfire would be visible for miles around and would pinpoint our position.' It seemed highly unlikely that the Japanese needed our position to be highlighted. They seemed to know exactly where we were, and there were enough

[39]

fires going for a couple more not to make any great difference. But I owed far too much to the Colonel to make me wish to oppose him on inessentials.

The Colonel was in favour of a mass grave being dug outside the town's perimeter. Then a local official – one of the few who had remained – pointed out rather stuffily that that would never do, as it would offend religious differences. There would be a riot if Buddhists were buried with Christians, or Muslims with Hindus. There would have to be separate pits.

Brocklehurst was as tired as the rest of us, and the fatigue was etched into his face, but his concern was for his men, who had had very little sleep for several days. Digging *one*, let alone several pits, would require untapped sources of hidden strength. Furthermore, he was not particularly impressed by religious niceties. 'Christ, man,' he complained to the official, 'we all go the same way when we die, don't we?' But he was always open to compromise: one big hole would be dug outside the town, but bamboo screens would be erected between the various races. Even in death there could never be unity in that divided land.

The soldiers' work carrying the putrefying corpses to their last resting place made my own efforts in transporting the wounded from one hospital to another look very puny. They used their own transport to carry the bloated, evil-smelling remains to the massive hole which it had taken them all night to dig. The stench was so sickeningly overpowering that they worked with cloths soaked in disinfectant wrapped round their mouths. Many of the bodies were so decomposed and mutilated that it was impossible to compile a proper list of the dead. The scene was made even more macabre by about fifty local people, who squatted by the hole wailing their grief. They were supposed to help with the digging, instead they were a ruddy nuisance.

Vultures hovered hopefully in the nearby trees, but they were made to look dignified by the antics of some human birds of prey who, whenever anyone's back was turned, took the opportunity to deprive the dead of the tattered remnants of clothes clinging to their remains. They also pulled off the small trinkets and charms that were going to be buried with their former owners. A guard was mounted that night to prevent these ghouls from digging up remains, but there was no way of dispersing the packs of starving wild dogs which prowled at a discreet distance from the perimeter of the crater. Occasionally one of them, ribs protruding like a scrubbing board, would become so emboldened at the sight of so much carrion that it slunk through and darted off with a chunk of human flesh to which clung a few shreds of cloth. They were indifferent to the boots and rifle butts aimed at them, and their lips curled back, exposing yellow teeth in a snarl of defiance. I told the soldiers to let them make off with their gruesome haul. 'We have enough problems on our hands without adding rabies to them, and that's what we'll have if anyone gets bitten,' I said.

I had spent a number of years in India and was accustomed, if not immune, to seeing the dead piled high after famines and epidemics, and the vultures and hyenas bloated through feasting on them. But I could see from their faces that, battle-hardened as they were, the soldiers were sickened at what they were witnessing. Even more incomprehensible to them was the conduct of the natives towards their own dead, and they made no attempt to conceal their horror and contempt. 'Worse than bloody animals,' snarled one private. It was useless to try to tell him that in the Far East life was very cheap. In any case, I did not have time to indulge in explanation, and I wasn't too concerned about offending anyone's humanitarian instincts. I simply wanted to see the bodies buried before plague broke out. As far as I was concerned, the dead owed the living something. It was almost dark before we completed the grisly task, but at least the corpses were deep enough down to dissuade anyone from disturbing their peace.

Some of the soldiers were so revolted by what they had seen that they formed up next morning for an impromptu sick parade outside the dispensary, asking for something to settle their queasy stomachs.

If there was anybody who deserved a medal for acting beyond the call of duty and observing the highest tradition of the nursing service, it was those six lads who, before they were ordered to report to me, could not distinguish a fibia from a tibia. Yet they were ready to tackle anything, learned with astonishing speed, and before long were helping set broken limbs and perform minor operations. Towards the end, they even gave a hand with major surgery.

The cheerful Cockney sergeant was heroic in his efforts, although I must confess he sometimes irritated me almost beyond endurance. He knew my name was Helen, but he insisted on calling me Florence, which after a time he abbreviated to Flo. I suppose it was his way of showing his respect for what I had been trying to do, but I had no wish at all to be compared with the lady with the lamp. I admit, though, that when I cast my eyes around the wards I often reflected that conditions in the Crimea could hardly have been any worse. Later I discovered that the sergeant believed I did not appreciate the reason for his leg pulling. He thought the only nightingale I knew was the song bird, and took my irritation for a proof of my ignorance of history.

One evening after a particularly hectic day, Annie came to me and whispered that there was a terrible moaning sound coming from the direction of the main entrance. I went out to investigate. As I did not dare to use a torch or a lamp, I could only rely on my sense of hearing, so I paused and waited for the moaning to start again, then moved towards it. Eventually I traced the groans to a pile of rubble and there found an elderly, emaciated man with mongoloid features, lying in the shelter of the ruined outhouse. In the dim light I recognised him as someone I had known for many years; he used to have a sweet stall on bazaar day and as a girl I had been a regular customer. He was obviously badly hurt, although I could not see the extent of his injuries. I summoned help and we carried him into one of the wards where I could examine him. He was in a pitiful state; one of his legs was shattered and gangrene had set in. He wasn't sure how long before he had been injured, for he had frequently lapsed into unconsciousness, but he recalled being hit by something when the planes first attacked the market square. Somehow or other he had managed to crawl to his village, only to find it was deserted. With no home to return to, no family or friends to succour him, the only place he could think of where help might be found was my hospital.

After I had washed him and cleansed his shattered leg, he looked at me with imploring eyes and said in his broken English: 'Can you help me?'

I looked down at him and replied as gently as I could: 'I will try, but you are very ill. We have no doctors here and you need an operation.'

He insisted on knowing exactly what I meant. I suppose that death had become so commonplace that I had developed a callousness I would have deplored a few days before, but I honestly could not see any point in withholding the truth. He had all the stoicism of an old man who had faced death and was no longer afraid of it. I felt he deserved a wholly honest verdict. If conditions had been different, I might have sat by his bedside until death brought a merciful release, but the cries and groans around me reminded me that there were others in great need too. So I said bluntly, 'A surgeon must amputate – cut off your leg – or you will die. But we do not have a surgeon here. If I tried to do it, you would die anyway.'

His wrinkled face was expressionless as he replied: 'If you are your father's daughter, you will cut off my leg.'

I walked out into the open and began to weep quietly, then to pray. I paced up and down trying to make up my mind what to do, but I knew in my heart that there would be no miraculous voice from heaven to guide me. The decision must be mine, and mine alone. As I went back to the ward I half hoped to find that he had resolved my problem by passing peacefully away. But he was conscious and coherent. 'Will you do it?' he asked. I simply

[43]

nodded my head. If he had such faith in me, I had to make the attempt to justify it.

I went into the operating theatre, sat down, and tried to recall everything I have heard or read about amputations. I realised it was not an awful lot, and I did not even have an article in a magazine to help me as had happened with the unexploded bomb. There was no point in hesitating, however; delay could only make things worse. I stood up and called for the sergeant. When he came in I said, with a brusqueness and confidence I did not feel: 'I want you to help me prepare the theatre for an amputation.' I could hear my own voice and it sounded as if I was talking about something I did every day of the week. The dear sergeant was very far from being taken in, however; from the look on his face I could see that he expected the roof to cave in any moment. But all he said was: 'Just tell us what to do, Flo. I'm game for a try.'

I asked him if any of his men had any knowledge of administering an anaesthetic, and he shook his head. 'But we learn quickly,' he said with a wry grin.

I tried to sound cool and in control as I shouted orders for gallons of water to be boiled, and all the instruments I would require to be sterilised. The theatre was thoroughly scrubbed out before the patient was wheeled in, lifted on to the operating table and tied down. I warned the lads that he might struggle violently if the anaesthetic did not work too well. The curtains were drawn and the lights switched on. The only person who seemed calm and composed was the old man, who had sufficient courage and faith to entrust his life to a couple of soldiers who had been trained to kill, and a nurse who would have had trouble threading a needle – her hands were shaking so much.

I cleaned the leg with alcohol, and then gave the patient a morphine injection. I had rigged up a primitive chloroform drip, as it was out of the question to try and use anything more sophisticated. I now handed this to one of the soldiers, showed him how it worked, then said firmly: 'Don't let him come round at any cost.'

[44]

I looked at the pale and apprehensive young men and warned them: 'This is going to be pretty gruesome, so I don't want either of you passing out on me.' What I did not say was that I was in no better state than they were. Fainting was my own greatest fear.

We donned our masks and I marked out the area for the incision, then asked the sergeant to hand me a knife from the sterilising steam box. I muttered a silent prayer and began to cut through the blackened flesh. I could see that the sergeant, who was operating the drip, was doing his utmost to keep control of himself; he succeeded triumphantly and his hand never faltered. Then I reached the bone and asked for the saw. It proved much harder work cutting through it than I had expected, and I suddenly became aware that two hands were on the handle. The sergeant was lending me some much-needed assistance.

I could see the beads of sweat on the foreheads of the soldiers and I knew they were making a superhuman effort. Perhaps, as with me, the knowledge that a human life was in their hands had given them an inner strength. When my saw was almost through I called out for a bucket; I was overcome by nausea as the severed limb fell with a dull plop. I realised too late that not to have eaten for several days was a distinct disadvantage when tackling a major operation. But the worst part was over and I began to put on sutures and a stump dressing. The sergeant, although looking very green, was still helping me. The other soldier had passed out.

I shook him: 'Wake up and help us get him back to bed!'

'I've killed men in battle,' he said apologetically, 'but I've never seen anything like that before.' I took the patient's pulse. Although it was far from healthy I at least knew he had survived his tremendous ordeal. There was life, so there must still be hope.

We wheeled him back to his bed and gently lifted him on to it. Then a soldier appeared at the bedside with three cups of steaming hot tea. 'Cuppa,' he said. 'You look like you could do with one.' The Tommies' time-worn remedy for all crises worked like a charm. I gulped it down, then fell asleep on the floor beside the old man's bed.

I don't know how long I slept before his stirrings woke me. When I stood up I could see that he was feeling for his non-existent limb. But there was no emotional outburst, instead he looked at me and said: 'I prayed to God that you would help me. I am determined to live, missy. I will not die.'

It occurred to me that I did not even know his name. That hardly seemed to matter, nothing would have changed if I had. Yet the fact seemed somehow to underline the extraordinary nature of what we had just done. Briskly I said, 'I've got work to do. I can't stand here chattering,' and I turned away and instructed the sergeant and his theatre assistant to take the leg outside and burn it.

That night I sat in my room, wishing there was some way in which I could express my deep thanks, and my admiration for these young men who had travelled half way across the world to fight for a land that had previously only existed for them in a school atlas, and who had done so much more than their duty. I had nothing to offer them, and mere words seemed a poor reward. Then I remembered that a handful of members still frequented the Club, with its well-stocked bar. I had no idea why they clung on; I suppose it had become such a part of their life they could not alter it – rather like members of an endangered species that faces extinction but refuses to adapt in order to survive. They would surely be able to help.

I walked up to the Club through the empty, still smouldering streets, and went through the door into the bar. A few figures sat huddled in wicker chairs, the male equivalent of Miss Havisham, mourning a past that had gone forever. I sought out a committee member and said I would like a few bottles of beer for my soldiers. As briefly as I could I told him what they had been doing. He looked acutely embarrassed and said: 'I'm afraid that isn't possible, Miss Rodriguez. This club is for officers only.' I left the drink he had offered me untouched on

Studio portrait of me with my mother

My first home, the civil surgeon's house at Taunggyi

Mr White, my pet buffalo

Craigmore

the table, and stormed out without saying a word.

Late that same night I invited my commandos to join me on a 'secret mission', hastily adding that it was one I thought they would enjoy. I got them to collect the zinc bath tubs we used for washing down the less sick patients, and together we headed through the dark streets to the Club. I did not tell the soliders what I had in mind, for although law for the civilian population had ceased to exist, the army still had its own strict discipline. The less they knew about what they were going to do, the better. They were baffled but, as always, ready to oblige. As far as I was concerned, I could place my hand on my pounding heart and solemnly declare, 'I am doing no great wrong.' In any case, there is nothing quite like the sweet taste of revenge.

I had known the Club since I was old enough to sit on the veranda and sip an ice-cold lemonade, and so I could almost walk blindfold to the door of the store room at the back of the premises. I had armed myself with a native *dah*, a particularly lethal looking knife, and with it easily prised off the padlock and opened the door. A treasure house of 'goodies' was spread out before us: beer, spirits, cleaning powders and liquids, and a rare luxury – toilet paper. In a whisper I told the soldiers to fill up the bath tubs with everything they could lay their hands on. I got particular pleasure from seeing one of the men pick up a crate of whisky, which was marked for personal delivery to the Club Secretary.

When we had helped ourselves to all we could carry we set off back to the hospital. If anyone had spotted us they would have scratched their heads in amazement; Taunggyi had been the scene of some odd-looking processions in the past few days, but nothing quite so incongruous as ours as it threaded its way gingerly through the debris-littered streets. I put a huge bundle on my head, and a basket in each hand, while the soldiers were labouring under the burden of the heavy bath tubs.

Once we had reached the safety of the hospital I invited the soldiers into my quarters where I served them with whatever they fancied – whisky, gin, or beer. The look on their faces was

[47]

one of delight, mingled with disbelief. Although it could hardly be described as a hectic orgy, the soldiers had a good time and slept all the better for it. Next day I announced that some beer or spirits would be issued every day, but that it would be strictly rationed. We hid our ill-gotten gains under the stilts on which my quarters stood, and waited to see if anyone found out about our raid.

Next day the penitent committee member called to see me. Unlike us he had obviously had a sleepless night, mulling over his refusal to serve non-commissioned ranks. 'I should have let you have it,' he lamented. 'Looters broke in last night and almost emptied the place. I would have much preferred your chaps to have had it than them.'

Tongue-in-cheek I expressed my sympathy, but felt it might be indiscreet to offer him a drink by way of consolation.

The commandos were still busy with their campaign of demolition. As time was running out my helpers were often called away to help, which meant they seldom got any real sleep, and the burden of their work in the hospital became still more onerous. They never flinched. Then, on the evening of 20th April, the Government officers left, and British civil administration came to an end. No one could blame them, for to remain any longer would have meant certain capture and internment.

I knew then that it could not be long before the moment arrived that I had been secretly dreading: the commando unit would receive orders to pull out. The Japanese were now very close, and apart from continuing the policy of destruction as they retreated, Colonel Brocklehurst's men had been given another vitally important task: the spiriting away of a vast fortune before the enemy could seize it. The princes of the Shan States were Midas-rich, much of their wealth coming from the immensely profitable opium trade. As a child I had witnessed how they ostentatiously displayed their fortunes at official functions: umbrella handles studded with rare gems, costumes blazing with diamonds, sapphires and rubies. The civil administration in Taunggyi acted as trustees for the funds of the princes, and these still reposed, in the form of fourteen tons of notes, rare jewels and bullion, in the cellars of Government House. It would be a rich and easily negotiable haul for the enemy if they could lay their hands on it, and although the notes could be burned, there was no way of destroying the silver, jewels and valuable coinage. There had already been attempts made to loot the treasure-house, some of them partially success-ful, and the authorities decided that before the rest of it disappeared, they would like it to be evacuated and used as a contribution to the Allied rather than the Japanese war effort. It is one of the hard facts of war that cash is every bit as important as bullets; in fact, you can't have one without the other, unless you are lucky enough to find a people as generous as the Americans to help you with the essentials.

I learned about their special mission from the soldiers, and so was not surprised when Colonel Brocklehurst turned up one morning and announced that they were leaving. I heard my Cockney sergeant say with obvious concern: 'What about Flo, sir?' adding hastily 'and the hospital?' Even in that moment of crisis he still declined to call me Helen.

The Colonel took me aside and tried to convince me of the folly of remaining. He did his utmost to make me agree, pointing out the appalling dangers I would be running and the improbability that the Japanese would let me continue with my work even if I stayed behind. Obstinately I insisted I just couldn't down tools and walk out on the patients. I sensed that he knew I was right, for he gave up pleading.

Later, however, he returned to the charge. This time he changed his tactics and curtly told me that I *was* leaving. That was an order. Then he handed me a khaki shirt and pair of slacks and instructed me to cut my hair off. I suppose he expected me to pass myself off as a soldier. I mumbled some-thing about having taken vows, but he was unmoved. 'You have got ten minutes to get ready,' he snapped.

'I don't need ten minutes, or ten days for that matter!' I

retorted. 'My mind is made up. Please go.' He knew there was no point in arguing further and I could see how concerned he was about me. 'I feel as if I am leaving a daughter behind,' he said.

I jerked my head in the direction of the hospital. 'I think of them as my family now. They are helpless, if I left them they would die.'

He pursed his lips, paused, then said: 'Do you realise what you are exposing yourself to? You could be raped, tortured, killed.' He glanced at his watch and told me time was nearly up. This was my last chance. I can't help smiling now when I think of the pompous and stilted words which for some reason came to my lips. 'I absolve you from all responsibility. You have done all you can to make me change my mind. You can leave with a clear conscience.'

My words brought the suggestion of a smile to his face, as he remarked, with some feeling: 'You are a remarkable young lady, you know.'

I smiled in return. 'I'll take my chances here.'

'You are very young. Can you stand it?'

'I will have to. But stop worrying about me. *You* might not make it!'

Years were to pass before I learned how painfully true my last casual remark was to prove. Only two or three of them did in fact survive. Colonel Brocklehurst and most of his men perished: either shot, drowned, or dead of sickness and malnutrition. Thankfully, my sergeant was one of those who survived. When I made my slightly callous comment, I had meant it as a joke, for I honestly did not believe that anyone or anything could ever defeat those men or quench their indomitable strength and courage.

Like so many others in Burma, some lie in unmarked graves, while others have no grave at all. When the war ended I tried to find out what had happened to the fortune which had been given them to protect, but it seems to have vanished without trace. Presumably the Japs got it, or it was seized by dacoits. It may even have been buried, and, like so much of Burma's treasure, never recovered. During the evacuation, many families buried their most precious possessions and Regiments their silver. All hoped to return one day to reclaim it. Few did. Beneath the soil of Burma today lies an El Dorado, waiting for some lucky peasant to stumble on it.

But I digress.

The sergeant came down to see me one last time before the unit pulled out. He arrived in a battered and rusty black Ford sedan which he had found at the end of a mud track where its driver had abandoned it. I was busy cleaning the operating theatre when I heard his boots thump along the veranda. 'I thought you'd gone,' I said.

'We're just moving off, Flo. We won't be back.'

I looked at his battered little car and dredged up a smile. 'I see you'll be travelling in comfort, sergeant.'

'It's for you, Flo. I've borrowed it. But there's still time for you to change your mind and hop on one of our lorries.'

I shook my head and left it at that.

He told me to hide the car around the back of the hospital. When the Japanese arrived I was to pack it as full as I could with passengers, and then drive off as fast and as far as I could.

'I hope you've left a key with it.'

'There isn't one. I fixed up the ignition with some bits of wire. But it's got more than half a tankful of petrol. Get as far as you can with it.' He hesitated and murmured, 'And God bless you.'

'Goodbye, sergeant,' I said.

'Goodbye, sister.' Calling me that was the nicest compliment he could have paid me. I would have hated him to go and just leave Flo behind.

It was not the last I saw of the soldiers. Around dusk their 30-cwt. truck drove past the hospital and they waved to me. I knew they would be coming and had put on a clean white uniform, as I wanted to look my best and not present a picture of total dejection. I tried to smile as I returned their waves; then as the dust billowed up behind the truck I started to run towards it. I suppose I ran a few yards, then I stopped and walked slowly back to the wards.

Through the swirling dust above the tail board of the bucketing lorry, I could see the white teeth of the soldiers exposed in wide grins. I watched until they were out of sight. They were the last free men that I was to see for three and a half years.

Chapter 3

As I sat slumped and miserable on the veranda, a feeling of utter desolation engulfed me. This, I thought, must be how a solitary castaway must feel when marooned on a desert island, remote from the shipping lanes and with little or no chance of rescue. I was wallowing in a trough of self-pity and I knew it, even relished it. But it was a short-lived period of self-indulgence, for I soon reminded myself that the choice had been my own. I had been given ample opportunities to leave and I had turned them down. Self-pity gave way to shame. I reddened as I imagined Colonel Brocklehurst observing me unseen, reminding me of the words I had spoken so defiantly when he had urged me to leave.

I straightened my back and concentrated on what needed to be done. Nothing could disguise the fact that we were in a desperate plight. I had no contact with the outside world, and therefore no idea of how the war was progressing, but what at least was certain was that it was not going in our favour. I knew enough to understand that the next lot of uniforms I saw would not be worn by British soldiers. There was no point in looking for a dramatic rescue in that direction. I was on my own. Somehow or other I had to survive, for if I did not then neither would my patients. But how? I asked. And so like many others in times of despair, I lowered my head and prayed, silently reciting the words of 'A Nurse's Prayer', an illuminated copy of which hung above my bed. Not that I needed any visible reminder, for the words were indelibly printed in my memory; I had repeated them so often on occasions when I was besieged by doubt. What I now desperately needed was to be reminded of my reason for remaining in Taunggyi. I wanted the reassurance of knowing that I was doing the right thing, that there was nothing else I could have done.

Lord who on earth did minister to those who helpless lay,
In pain and weakness hear me now, as unto thee I pray.
Give to my eyes the power to see the hidden source of ill,
Give to my hand the healing touch, throb of pain to still.
Grant that mine ears be swift to hear the cry of those in pain,
Give to my tongue the words that bring comfort and strength again,
So in thy footsteps may I tread, strength in thy strength alway,
So may I do thy blessed work, and praise thee day by day.

It was a prayer that had sustained me in the past, when the words came easily to my lips and when I never really thought I would need to utter them in dire emergency. Now the emergency had come.

I felt a lot better after that. From a poetical point of view the prayer might not rank very high, but I was asking for what I needed most, not declaiming an epic piece of literature. That simple prayer brought me back to reality. There was a lot more to occupy my mind than my personal plight. There was a job to be done. Having addressed myself to the Almighty I gave myself a stiff dressing down and strode purposefully into the wards to commence my rounds.

I exuded a confidence I did not feel, for my prayer had not resulted in any immediate divine intervention. On the contrary, the suffering was still there and the anguished cries still strident. But I felt now that I would somehow find the strength to do what was needed. I paused at the foot of each bed, gave a banal little pep-talk to the occupant, and made it sound as if things had taken a turn for the better. 'At last we've been left alone, you'll be pleased to hear. Now I can concentrate on making you all well and getting you up and about again. But I can't help you as much as you can help yourself. Remember that.'

They were words that must have been uttered a million times

since the first nurse trod the first ward, but empty as they may have sounded to me they had a comforting effect. All sick people need encouragement and there is no finer medicine than to be told you are well on the way to recovery if you pull your socks up.

Having got that off my chest it was back to the endless routine. Wards were cleaned down, wounds dressed, medicine administered and food prepared. Although our diet was monotonous and unappetising, we were still far from starving, for I had hidden an emergency supply of food under a pile of firewood in the compound which would keep us going for some time.

Our store consisted of two cases of condensed milk, which were reserved for the mothers and babies, and three cases of vegetable soup, which I supplemented with some of the feed we had for the hens. It may not sound very appetising, admittedly, but many have survived and thrived on less. Not many of the patients can have been used to richer or more varied fare.

After the horrors we had experienced, the feeling of abandonment proved in some respects a welcome relief. We were granted a respite from the war. The Japanese must have known we were no longer a worthwhile target so that at least we were not continually running to the slit trenches or trying to carry the sick to places of relative safety. The eerie silence, oppressive though it might be, was preferable to the din of bombs and guns with its aftermath of shattered bodies and maimed minds.

Our period of tranquillity was brief. One morning, Annie came rushing in to inform me excitedly that two Burmese were acting in a very suspicious manner outside the hospital. I at once concluded that they were on the look out for anything they might be able to loot. I strode down the steps of the front porch with all the determination I could summon up, and demanded to know what they were doing on private property. The appearance of the two men was not particularly alarming, for they looked much like any other local native; their hair was long and they wore the traditional garb of the Burman: a long jacket over a *loongyi*. They meekly said that they were hungry and looking for something to eat.

As soon as they opened their mouths I knew that they were not Burmese, for they spoke the language with a very peculiar accent. Now I began to feel really nervous. I did my utmost to conceal my fear, however, and told them that they would have to apply elsewhere as we were desperately short of food and what we had was needed for the patients. The explanation fell on deaf ears. They kept walking towards me, then suddenly broke into a run, seized hold of me and pounced on Annie who was standing just behind. One grabbed hold of Annie's neck and forced her to the ground while the other snatched at my arm and began to twist it up behind my back. The pain was excruciating and I screamed out: 'If you touch either of us, I will shoot you.' The threat merely provoked a burst of laughter, indeed we had so clearly been touched already that I found it slightly ridiculous myself. I could see that the man who had Annie on the ground was trying to strangle her, and from the pressure being exerted on my arm I knew that my assailant was determined to break it and render me helpless. But I still had one hand free.

Shortly before he left, Jock Garratty had insisted on presenting me with a .38 pistol. Though he did not say so in so many words I think he intended that I should use it on myself if the Japanese captured me and seemed set on rape. I had heard that Europeans often gave this advice to their womenfolk, feeling that to be ravished – especially by an Oriental – was so obviously a fate worse than death that the fact required no arguing. My own views on the problem were slightly different but I had accepted the pistol. I had only a rudimentary knowledge of its working but I was prepared to try to protect myself if I had to, and the mere sight of the weapon would usually be enough to deter a marauder. I had taken to carrying the pistol in the back pocket of my slacks, hardly giving it a thought and certainly never expecting to have to use it in earnest. Now the unexpected had happened. With my free hand I reached round and pulled out the pistol.

Annie was screaming and struggling on the ground, and as I raised the gun I was desperately afraid of hitting her. Suddenly the man's head was clear of her. I pulled the trigger. The explosion was deafening. I felt the blast against my face and could smell the acrid odour of the explosive. I feared that I would miss but more by luck than expert marksmanship, my bullet took the top of his head off. As he toppled back, Annie clambered to her feet and rushed forward to help me. The shock of seeing his partner in villainy drop dead made my attacker momentarily release his grip. His face was only inches away when I pulled the trigger for a second time. It disintegrated before my eyes, like a squashed over-ripe melon, and I was smothered in blood and pulped bone.

The gun dropped from my fingers and I stood there sobbing and shaking uncontrollably. I could not bring myself to look down at my handiwork. Violent death is always a loathsome spectacle and doubly so when you are responsible for it. I was stricken with a feeling of remorse and guilt. I had dedicated my life to saving people and, not so long ago, had reaffirmed that pledge in prayer, yet here I was a murderess. I was assailed with agonising doubt. Were they really the killers I had supposed them to be? Had I shot two men for no other reason than that they were hungry?

I became aware of Annie shouting excitedly, almost hysterically. I turned towards her and saw that she was kneeling down beside one of the corpses whose jacket she had ripped open, pointing at the green-coloured tunic she had exposed. 'Look, look! They're Japanese soldiers. Don't waste tears on them. They are filthy dogs!'

Although I had been taught to believe that all life is sacred, my relief at hearing her words was total. I knelt beside the other soldier, opened the blouse and saw that he too wore some kind of insignia on his uniform tunic. I had no idea what it meant, but I did know he was Japanese and I shook off my feeling of guilt with the ease of a snake shedding its skin. I began to wonder what they were doing dressed up as Burmese peasants, and concluded that they must be the advance party of a Japanese column, which had been sent ahead to reconnoitre the area and make sure it was clear of enemy troops before the main body moved in. If my assumption was correct it meant the Japanese forces could not be far away. It would not be long before they put in an appearance, and when they did and found the bodies of their dead comrades Annie and I would be shot out of hand. It was a chilling thought but I managed not to panic. There was no time to waste.

'We must get rid of them, Annie,' I said. 'We must leave no trace that they were ever here.' I sounded a lot calmer than I felt, for in my imagination I could already hear the tramp of marching feet. Annie nodded agreement and we each took a leg and dragged one of the bodies towards a small slit trench. The head bounced along the ground, leaving a grisly smear of blood in the dust. As we hauled our burden towards the ready-made grave, which not so long ago had been a means of saving life, jewellery and money began to spill out of the pockets; obviously items the Japanese scout had looted from abandoned houses. Annie promptly dropped the leg she was holding and began to pick up coins and jewellery. 'We may need this to buy things with,' she said in a practical voice. Angrily I told her to stuff it all back in the pockets. 'We'll manage without it,' I snapped.

When we had tumbled the corpse into the trench we went back to collect the other one and repeated the process. Then we stood back, panting heavily as we surveyed our handiwork. The two bodies lay in grotesque disjointed postures at the bottom of the trench. I shouted to Annie to help me collect a load of firewood and some cans of kerosene so that we could burn the corpses and destroy all trace of the visit. Sweat drenched us as we hastily piled twigs and firewood over the bodies, all the time anxiously glancing over our shoulders for the arrival of the Japanese troops.

When the bodies were completely covered we doused the wood with drums of kerosene and set fire to it. We soon discovered that burning a human body is an extremely difficult task, far more so than reducing it to a corpse in the first place. The flames roared high, but when they died down the bodies were still clearly recognisable. We piled on more wood and carpeted it with leaves so as to retain the heat, then emptied more drums of kerosene. Still the evidence of our crime remained. Eventually we resorted to using anything that was inflammable, including huge drums of cooking oil. After what seemed an eternity only a black and charred mess remained. We filled in the trench and smoothed over the surface to remove all signs that it had ever existed. Finally we raked over the surface of the compound so as to remove the incriminating blood trail along which we had dragged the bodies.

By then I was completely exhausted and could scarcely remain on my feet. Annie supported me back to the veranda, where I slumped down on to a seat. Apart from the mental strain of what we had just done, I was in poor physical shape, for some time before I had removed the bullet or piece of shrapnel which had been embedded in my calf, and had made a complete hash of the operation. As a result the large hole was infected and I was running a high fever. But I was consoled by the thought that all traces of the crime had been removed. Even if the Japanese dug up the whole compound they would find only the decomposing remains of those who had died from sickness or through their own bombs and bullets. There would be no trace of their missing comrades, unless they could identify them by the coins and baubles which they had stolen.

I had little time to torture myself about the immensity of my crime, or for that matter to give a thought to my physical condition. A major distraction came in the form of a massive artillery exchange between the Japanese and Chinese as they fought for control of Taunggyi. The Chinese troops were part of Chiang Kai-shek's army, which had been fighting the Japanese long before Britain declared war on Japan. They were, I knew, our allies, but from the little I had heard of their exploits, no one to date had been particularly impressed by their contribution to the war effort. They were said to be brave and good fighters, but with little discipline and ᴀs ready to loot and murder among the Burmese as to engage the real enemy. Whatever the truth of this, what was painfully clear as I stood quaking on the veranda was that we were 'piggy in the middle' in the soulless game of war. I had no idea, as the earth trembled and shells whined and whistled overhead, that the Chinese were fighting a bitter delaying action as they tried to withdraw relatively intact into China in the face of a Japanese army that had routed the British and had now set its sights on the prized goal of India.

For the next three days and nights the opposing forces shelled each other across the already devastated town. During the daytime one could see the huge puffs of smoke rising up from distant crags, followed by reverberating crashes as the shells exploded. But if the days were unnerving, the nights were still more so, for then the skies were illuminated by bright lightning flashes, followed by the deafening detonation of shells whose destination one could only guess at. Several landed near the hospital and caused further damage to the already battered buildings, and once again the wards echoed to the screams of helpless people who, confined to their beds, could only cower in terror and hope for the best. Annie and I, with the help of the remaining Gurkha servants, did what we could to ease their suffering, but it did not amount to much. Shell splinters whizzed through the shattered windows and three people were killed and several more wounded. To add to our problems several water pipes were shattered and we had to cope with the additional hazard of widespread flooding.

Then as abruptly as it had started the barrage stopped. For a moment or two the uncanny silence was even more unnerving than the ceaseless bombardment to which we had been subjected. But with the respite we were able to bury the dead, attend to the wounded, and provide meals for those who had escaped physically, if not mentally intact. Everyone was suffering from nervous exhaustion which a feeling of our complete inability to do anything to protect ourselves, still less to affect the course of events, did nothing to relieve. I had been amazed, again and again, at what the human frame could endure, but I knew there had to come a time when we could take no more.

Lack of sleep had worn us out and it is well known that nothing lowers morale more rapidly than total tiredness. Judgement is impaired and the making of the most simple decisions becomes a major effort. An alert and active mind can control an infected body, but the human brain is like a battery, it needs re-charging and if it is allowed to go flat everything fails to function. I knew that, so far as Annie and I were concerned, there must come a time when we could endure no more. It would have been unrealistic to imagine that such a time could be very far away. And if we succumbed, then so would our charges. We were the crutches on which they depended.

One can endure and survive so long as there is hope, but to us there seemed no flicker of light at the end of the long tunnel we were travelling. No sooner had we survived one ordeal than something fresh was inflicted upon us. What would happen next and would the next straw finally break us? It was a fear that nagged at me like the exposed nerve of an aching tooth.

When the next blow came it did not break us; in my case indeed it only strengthened my resolve to see things through to the bitter end. Nevertheless, it was a traumatic experience, made even more painful by the fact that it came from a most unexpected quarter. The last thing I had envisaged was that our lives would be endangered by our Chinese allies. A few hours after the firing ceased, I became aware of a sound that had long been missing in Taunggyi: voices raised in excited chatter. From my veranda I could see the odd fire springing up in different parts of the town, and I became aware of the drab-coloured figures moving stealthily along the streets and darting in and out of the shattered shops and houses. Then a horde of uniformed figures began approaching the hospital. They were obviously soldiers, for some carried rifles and automatic weapons, while others had long bamboo poles slung between their soldiers from which were suspended bundles of

[61]

all shapes and sizes. Those who were playing the part of coolies seemed little more than boys and as they got closer I thought they could be no more than fifteen or sixteen years old.

As they swarmed into the compound and headed towards me, I could not help reflecting that they looked a ragamuffin lot; their uniforms were almost in tatters and they seemed to have lost all semblance of discipline. For a moment I thought they must be brigands or dacoits, then it dawned on me that they were retreating Chinese, who were systematically looting what houses were still standing as they withdrew from the town. The shapeless bundles hanging from the bamboo poles were what they had managed to find in the already repeatedly pillaged homes, shops and godowns. As they emptied each building they set fire to it – either to deny shelter to the Japanese or out of sheer joy of destruction.

One of them advanced threateningly towards me. Although he wore nothing on his uniform that indicated his rank, I felt certain he must be an officer, for he brusquely gestured to some of the soldiers to take me inside the hospital. They broke into a run and prodded me in the back with their rifles. I led them to my own quarters as I did not want to alarm the patients. When we got into my sitting room two soldiers were posted at the door, while two more stood a few inches away, pointing their bayonets at my chest and another held a sharp knife against the back of my neck. The officer then screamed: 'You are a spy! You must tell me where the Japanese are.'

I realised that my appearance gave him some grounds for suspicion, for my build, height and complexion all made it obvious that I was not Burmese or Shan. I knew too that these men were probably as tired and frightened as I was, and that they would think nothing of taking my life unless I gave them some good reason for sparing me. With a knife pricking at my neck and two bayonets inches from my chest, it was extremely difficult to speak calmly, but I explained as best I could that I was in charge of the hospital and that I had not left with the other Europeans for the simple reason that there was no one

My father out with a shooting party

A typical pre-war fancy dress ball at Taunggyi. I am second from the left in the back row, supposedly disguised as an Arabian princess

Myself just before the outbreak of war

else to look after the sick. I knew nothing about the Japanese's whereabouts; our only preoccupation had been to try to escape their gunfire. My explanation did not seem to satisfy him at all, for he kept repeating the same question, his voice growing more and more menacing: 'You are a spy! Tell me where the Japanese are.' It crossed my mind that if I had not cremated the two soldiers I would have been able to provide ample evidence that I was anything but a spy. My caution had rebounded on myself.

The interrogation lasted for a good half hour, although the Chinese did not resort to physical violence. Their leader simply kept shouting his accusation parrot-fashion, as if repetition would make it true and persuade me to admit the fact. Eventually another soldier entered the room and mumbled something in Chinese. I could not understand what he said, but suspect he told the officer that my story was true – the place *was* a hospital. Whatever it was he said brought the interrogation to an abrupt halt and the soldiers began systematically to loot my quarters. What they did not want they smashed, the rest they crammed into sacks which were added to the spoils tied on to the bamboo poles. One of the soldiers picked up a bottle of Worcestershire Sauce and, thinking it was saki or some other form of alcohol, downed it in a gulp. Even in the nerve-racking situation in which I found myself I could not help smiling as he spat out the sauce, his face distorted into a grimace of distaste. Through the open window I could see more soldiers moving from building to building and ransacking everything they could find before setting fire to them. The store room was looted and they unearthed the hidden supply of milk and soup. Others were rounding up the hens and plucking them while they were still alive.

The soldiers suddenly left my room and ran into a half-demolished house in the next compound. There they barricaded themselves, and began to fire in the direction in which they thought the Japanese must be.

I stood alone in my room, thankful that I had escaped unhurt

[63]

and wondering how long it would be before the Chinese and Japanese fought a pitched battle around the hospital. When that happened we would be trapped with no hope of escape. I heard a loud whining at the door and opened it. One of my dogs, Lassie, a cross between a spaniel and a sheep dog, crept in and lay at my feet, as if saying she would protect me from any further attacks. She was a particularly vicious animal, whose temperament had not been mellowed by the fact that she was hungry and nursing five puppies. For some reason, she had taken to me, though; indeed, I was the only person who could control her at all. I was to owe my life to her savage nature, for the door opened and a Chinese soldier entered, promptly holding a knife to my throat. I had no chance to ask what he wanted as the dog began snarling and growling. I grabbed hold of her collar so as to try to restrain her, but she was too strong for me and hurled herself at the soldier's throat. His face froze into a mask of fear and he slashed down with his knife, inflicting a deep wound that ran down from the back of Lassie's neck to the shoulder blades. But the dog had him by the throat and blood spurted out, covering me, the animal and the walls. The man dropped his knife and tried to pull the dog away, but she refused to loosen her grip. He staggered backwards through the door and tumbled down the veranda steps into the dust outside, where he died in agony, choking on his own blood.

Gruesomely horrible though the incident had been, I still had enough self-control to think to myself that my luck must now surely run out. When the other Chinese saw their dead comrade they would kill me without a moment's hesitation. But as suddenly as they had arrived the soldiers departed. They fired a few more desultory shots, then began running off towards the convent and Craigmore. Despite their hasty retreat they still managed to do a bit more looting on the way and carry out the occasional act of arson.

Lassie was in fearful pain from her wound, but she let me stitch it up with an ordinary needle and thread, which was all I had as the hospital's supply of surgical thread had long since been exhausted. Then I gave her some aspirin in warm milk and let her sleep. Although Lassie was not one of my own dogs – she had been dumped on me by a fleeing family – she was extremely devoted and almost human in her understanding. When I was unable to visit my father she used to deliver notes to him which I attached to her collar. I did not put her chances of survival very high, but surprisingly, the huge blanket stitches all took and she got better. Alas, it was not for long. Later, when the Japanese were trying to exterminate the dog population, they paid soldiers for every tail they produced. I taught her to go into hiding whenever I shouted 'Jap', but although she managed to elude the dog-hunters she could not escape rabies and in the end I had to put her down.

I hurried back into the wards although my thoughts were really with my father. I wondered what would happen to him when the Chinese reached his home, but there was nothing I could do to help. It would have meant certain death if I had gone up to Craigmore to find out, and there was no Lassie to send with a message. I simply offered a silent prayer and hoped that they would spare an old and sick man.

There was no time anyway to dwell on the possibilities of what might happen to him for my ears caught the sound of voices raised excitedly in what I realised was a completely different language. I went outside and saw a group of Japanese soldiers moving towards my quarters. They were led by an immaculately uniformed officer wearing highly polished thigh boots and carrying a large sword at his side. He spoke perfect English and introduced himself as Lieutenant Tobayashi. He had only uttered a few words before I realised that his mind was working on the same lines as the departed Chinese. 'You are English, and you are a woman. Why are you here alone? You are a spy.'

Unlike the Chinese officer, my new accuser spoke quietly and with great courtesy. He sounded as if he were stating an established fact, something so obvious that it needed no proving. I was almost ready to believe what he said myself!

[65]

There was none of the aggressiveness which had marked my earlier interrogation, which struck me as rather ironic since the Chinese were supposed to be our allies and the Japanese our deadly enemies.

I replied as indignantly as I could: 'If I was a spy, I would not be foolish enough to remain here. I am a nurse.'

'You are telling lies. Where are your patients?'

'If you will follow me, I will show you.'

The lieutenant nodded stiffly and told me to lead the way. He followed me across the compound into the hospital and walked straight-backed between rows of beds. When he came to the foot of the one occupied by the elderly Chinese who had helped me rescue the soldiers from the military hospital, the man sat up and shouted: 'Leave her alone! She is a nurse. She looks after anyone who is sick. I am Chinese. I am your enemy. Kill me, but do not harm her.'

The lieutenant did not reply but simply jerked his head, indicating that I was to follow him. We returned to my quarters and he questioned me closely about the work I had been doing. He listened most attentively to all I said and then solemnly drew out his sword and saluted, saying: 'You are a very brave woman. I honour and respect you and I will see that you are not harmed in any way.' He was, he explained, the officer commanding the troops which had occupied Taunggyi, and he would issue orders that I was not to be disturbed at my work. He asked me for some paper and, when I produced it, took out his fountain pen and wrote two notices in Japanese. He then took an empty kerosene tin, split it in half with his sword, and pasted a notice on each side. One, he said, was to be placed outside the hospital; the other outside my quarters. 'Put a lantern beside each one so that they can be read at night. None of my soldiers will interfere with you once they have read what I have written.'

When I complimented him on his excellent English, he told me that he had been educated in Europe. This perhaps explained why he did not display the same callousness and

[66]

indifference to suffering as I was later to experience from Japanese who had never left their native soil, and had become imbued with the philosophy which was to make them even more hated than the Nazis. But despite his civilised approach he was a dedicated soldier, and he was determined to contribute to the Japanese dream of the total conquest of the Far East. He genuinely saw himself as the liberator of a down-trodden people.

He was very solicitous when I told him about my leg wound, and said he would see to it that a doctor came along to treat it. He went on to ask if there were any other Europeans in Taunggyi. I replied that there might be a priest and some French nuns at the convent, as I had seen smoke rising from one of the chimneys. He asked me how to get there, and when I had directed him he stood up, clicked his heels and strode out. Soon afterwards he returned with the Mother Superior. He was chatting with her in fluent French, and told me that he had given her the same guarantee of protection as he had given to me.

Lieutenant Tobayashi was a man of his word, for next morning an army doctor came to the hospital to look at my leg. After he had treated it, he asked if I could possibly help to mend his spectacles which had been broken during the advance. I told him I had no experience as an optician, although the out-patients department did possess equipment for testing eyes. He said that any glasses would be better than none, and that he was quite happy for me to give him whatever sort of hit-and-miss eye test I thought I could manage. So he patiently sat in a chair muttering, 'See, no see. See. No see,' while I slotted different lenses into the testing machine. Eventually, by a process of trial and error, he decided on the lenses which seemed to suit him best. I fitted these inside his old shattered frames, and tied them in position as best I could with some pieces of wire. It was a good turn that I was never to regret, for the doctor turned out to be a man who put his profession before dreams of conquest or the strict rules of military discipline.

[67]

Lieutenant Tobayashi and the doctor proved to me that one can never write off an entire nation as being composed of inhuman beasts. They treated me with generosity and consideration, and did their best to ensure that my work could continue uninterrupted. Their best was not always good enough, however as I was to find to my cost when the lieutenant's vigilance lapsed and exposed me to great danger.

One evening around five o'clock, as I was preparing food for the patients, two soldiers patrolling on bicycles rode up to the hospital, dismounted and marched into the kitchen. Presumably they had been drinking, for without warning they drew their bayonets and rushed at me. I was taken completely unawares and had no time to escape.

I had no idea what they hoped to achieve by their attack; perhaps they intended rape, a not uncommon pastime of drunken Japanese soldiers. Whatever the reason, they hacked and jabbed at me with more vigour than skill, while I kicked and punched out at them with all the strength I could summon. It was inevitable that one of their blows would eventually strike home, and I felt a searing pain in my stomach. I put my hand over my abdomen, saw the blood gushing out through my fingers, and thought to myself: 'So this is what it's like to die.' I knew that I could not defend myself and at any moment expected one of the bayonets to inflict a mortal wound. Then I heard Lieutenant Tobayashi's voice calling out my name.

Fortunately, so did the two soldiers, who rushed out of the building and scurried off as fast as they could. I had slumped down against the wall and was trying to stem the flow of blood when Tobayashi strode in with one of the nuns. Mercifully, she was a qualified nurse, who immediately rendered first aid, and assured me that although the stab wound looked very bad it was not all that serious; it had not penetrated the viscera and with a little careful nursing would soon heal.

Tobayashi was beside himself with rage and demanded to know where my two assailants had run off to. Annie, who had witnessed their hasty departure and was determined to see them punished, told him that they had run across the compound and were hiding behind a tall hedge. Bristling with rage, the lieutenant drew his sword and walked towards the hedge, where he halted and commanded the men to come out. They emerged shamefaced and cowed, in no manner resembling the ferocious thugs who had so savagely attacked me. Tobayashi ordered them to stand before him, and then began to flay them with the flat of his sword, and to kick them as if they were the lowest and most repulsive of animals. They took the merciless beating without showing the least sign of pain, although they presented a picture of abject humiliation when he ordered them to hand over their rifles and cycles and report back to headquarters, where he would deal with them later. I had learned that to deprive a Japanese soldier of his weapons was a great indignity, for only death should separate them, and the pain of this insult clearly registered on their faces. I never discovered what other punishment was meted out. No doubt if I had enjoyed a rather more saintly disposition I would have pleaded with the lieutenant for mercy on their behalf, but even in my wildest imaginings I have never set myself up as a saint and I am afraid I felt they deserved everything they got. Of one thing I was sure: if they survived they would never molest another woman again.

And so I found myself occupying a bed in my own hospital, but the wound was a superficial one and I was soon up and able to continue with my duties. While I lay in bed I recalled a story told by my mother, when I was a small child. I have no idea now why she told it to me, but I imagine it must have arisen out of some childish prank of mine in which I had managed to survive unhurt, when I clearly did not deserve to do so. For Mother said, 'You have a charmed life, Helen,' and went on to say that when my father went off to Mesopotamia at the beginning of the First War, she decided to take me home to her parents in Scotland.

We had sailed from Rangoon along with a number of other mothers with small children, in a ship of the Patrick Henderson

Line. The captain was apparently an extremely superstitious man, for when the ship was steaming through the Mediterranean, which was known to be infested with U-boats, he summoned the mothers together and asked if any of their children had been born with a caul – a tissue-paper-thin membrane which completely encompasses the baby at birth. My mother was surprised at the question, but announced that I had been born with one. Upon this the captain beamed with delight, and assured the rest of the mothers that they had nothing to fear from enemy submarines as the ship had a lucky talisman aboard – me. Of course, my mother, being a nurse and practically minded, took no notice of all this nonsense and assumed it was something the captain had dreamed up to give confidence to the anxious mothers. But that night the ship alongside was torpedoed and in the morning, despite a widespread search, no survivors were picked up. All that was to be seen were floating pieces of wreckage. The captain insisted that if I had not been aboard the torpedo would have struck us. My mother was unconvinced, but could not entirely suppress a sense of pride at my 'achievement'.

I have never been a superstitious person, but as I lay in the hospital bed and recalled the events that had occurred from the time the first bombs fell on Taunggyi and all the near escapes I had had, I crossed my fingers and told myself that maybe there was something in that old mariner's superstition. In any case, at that moment I was quite happy to believe there was. The way things were going it was obvious the war would last a long, long time and I could do with every slice of luck that might come my way.

Once I felt fit enough to make the effort, I asked to see Lieutenant Tobayashi. He readily agreed to the meeting, and I explained that I was desperately worried about my father who was elderly and sick and being cared for by some loyal servants at Craigmore. 'The last I saw of the Chinese soldiers when they left here, they were heading in the direction of his home. I'd like to go and see whether he is all right and bring him back here.'

Tobayashi paused and then shook his head. Such a request, he regretted, was impossible to grant; the house was in a closely guarded military area and had been sealed off with barbed wire. I persisted with my entreaties and he finally relented. He would, he said, arrange for a military vehicle to pick me up and drive me to Craigmore, but he warned me that his men would have their rifles trained on me in case I tried to escape or do anything foolish.

When a scout car came to pick me up I was ordered into the back, where I was hemmed in by armed soldiers and driven to the foot of the hill leading up to the house. As I began to walk up the steep slope I looked back and saw that the soldiers had dismounted and had aimed their rifles at me. For a horrifying moment, I thought they were going to open fire, but one of them gestured with his gun for me to keep moving.

As I approached the house I was struck by the uncanny silence that surrounded the rambling building, and I quickened my pace until I was running. My leg and stomach wound began to ache, but I had such a sense of impending doom that I ignored the pain and kept on up the slope. When I reached the compound my worst fears were realised. The place was in a shambles. Birds lay dead in their cages and the kennels were littered with the bodies of dogs which had died from starvation and thirst.

I called out, 'Father, are you all right?' but there was no response. Nervously I pushed open the front door and stepped inside, still calling out to him. The house had been ransacked. The furniture my parents had been so proud of had been smashed and burned, and the floors were littered with fragments of our once prized crockery. The teak mantelpiece, which my father had carved with such skill and patience, had been hacked and sawn to make crude rifle racks. All the silver was missing; the safe had been blown and the title deeds stolen. The floors and walls, which had been covered with beautiful pictures and carpets, were bare. I could not control my emotions and burst into tears. I knew that I would have to compose myself before I continued my tour of the house, and so I went out into the garden. The lawn was littered with bath tubs which had been ripped from their fittings and turned into makeshift boilers, and everywhere were the remains of bonfires from the cabinets and tables which had been lit so as to cook food.

As I stood looking at the remnants of our home, I heard a heartbreaking sound from the bottom kennel, and when I walked down I witnessed a most pitiful sight. Some of the dogs were still alive, but having been deprived of food and drink for many days, were running round and round in circles howling in agony. They were beyond rescue, and I knew that I would have to shoot them. For some unexplained reason, Tobayashi had not confiscated my revolver; for all I knew he was not even aware I possessed one. I hated the idea of putting a gun to the head of such old friends, but they had to be put out of their misery; one by one I shot them, then I turned away and went back into the house.

I went from room to room and the picture was always the same – everything movable had been looted, and what wasn't had been destroyed. I walked slowly up the stairs and went into my father's bedroom, still calling out to him. The room was completely bare except for a framed picture of Our Lord crucified, with the words, 'Come unto me' below his nailed feet. I retraced my steps into the garden and began to rummage among the piles of debris, looking for some small souvenir of Craigmore. I had almost given up hope of finding anything undamaged when I suddenly came across two perfect plates from Mother's 72-piece Crown Derby dinner and tea set. It had always been her proudest possession and was only brought out on special family occasions or when we were entertaining important guests. She treasured it so much she would never allow the servants to do the washing up, insisting on tackling it herself. I clasped the two plates to my breast and walked away, without even pausing to glance over my shoulder.

There was no point in lingering any longer. I had no idea where my father could be and there was no one there to ask. I stumbled blindly down the hill and clambered into the car, indicating to the soldiers that I wished to return to the hospital. I made no mention of my father, but simply said there were some mad dogs that had had to be destroyed. I do not know whether they had heard the shots or whether they reported them to Lieutenant Tobayashi. He chose never to refer to the matter if they did.

That night I walked across to the convent and unburdened my sorrows to the Mother Superior. She took my hand and we went into the chapel where we knelt together and asked the Good Lord to protect my father and the servants who had been with him, wherever they might be, and to return them safely to me.

Next day a Japanese officer called and politely requested the loan of a tray. I handed him my best lacquer one and asked him why he needed it. He proudly explained that a big parade was to be held on the town's sports ground to celebrate the occupation of the famous centre of Taunggyi. My tray was required to carry the proclamation scroll which had been sent by the Emperor, congratulating the soldiers on their famous victory. I was, he said, more than welcome to attend as a guest. I declined but said I would be most grateful if he would return my tray when he had finished with it.

That night I could not sleep. I stood on the veranda, gazing up towards Craigmore and wondering if my father had managed to elude the rampaging Chinese soldiers. As I looked towards my old home my thoughts automatically turned to my mother. I had no idea where she was either.

Through the moonlit darkness I saw a dark shape approaching, and for one heart-stopping moment I imagined it was my father. It was only the Japanese officer returning my tray. Somehow that small gesture summed up for me the futility of war. While some were celebrating, others were mourning; and yet even in those dark days I felt sure that the victory over which the Japanese were rejoicing would one day be wiped out in blood. No nation can gain out of war; it is just that some lose more than others.

Chapter 4

Days, then weeks, passed in painful suspense. Although I was kept continuously busy with my patients, my thoughts were always with my father. I had seen the wreckage of Craigmore, and I knew he would never have left the dogs in the pitiful condition in which I had found them: kennelled without water or food. But where had he been taken? I had no way of finding out. The entire area had been designated a military zone, and my movements were strictly limited. As if I did not have enough on my plate, I was now under pressure from Lieutenant Tobayashi to vacate the hospital, as most of the sick seemed on the road to recovery. Tobayashi told me he had been informed of this by the Japanese observer who made regular tours of the wards to note the condition of my patients.

I was determined to hang on; the last thing I wanted to do was move, for the hospital was the only address Dad had, and I knew if it was humanly possible he would get a message through. Somehow I had to find a good excuse for refusing to leave. It was not easy. I could not tell the truth and say that I was worried about my father for no one apart from me was interested in his fate, least of all the lieutenant. The length and breadth of Burma were littered with the corpses of refugees, the dusty roads and tracks dotted with unmarked graves; one more death made no difference to the victorious Japanese.

I sat down and pondered the problem for hour after hour, but no solution came to mind. Then I recalled the fear I had observed whenever the Japanese came into contact with contagious diseases; the mere mention of one was enough to send them scuttling off to a safe distance. No one deliberately risks infection but as a nurse I knew that, provided I took the necessary precautions, I was pretty safe. The Japanese, though, were petrified at the thought of being exposed. They set no store by precautions and knew of only one sure remedy; to put as much distance as possible between themselves and the sick. So I decided to have an outbreak of smallpox. I selected three fit and mobile patients whom I could trust implicitly, and dotted them from head to toes with micurochrome. Then I put them in a room on their own and stuck up a sign outside: 'Isolation Ward – Smallpox.'

When the observer arrived next day for his rounds, he immediately began his usual ploy of urging me to leave without delay. 'You are in the way here,' he said. I agreed with him and said nothing would please me more than to be relieved of my responsibilities. It just was not possible at the moment, though.

'You are always saying that,' he muttered angrily.

'Come with me and I will show you why,' I answered, with a mounting indignation that was as false as the spots on my three patients.

I led him to the door of the room, pointed at the sign and took him inside. He gave a quick look at the three victims and muttered one word: 'Pox.' My scarlet-painted patients looked really horrible, and they played their parts to perfection, groaning and thrashing around as I mumbled words of empty solace. The observer turned grey and fled off to his commanding officer. When he returned soon afterwards he would not come closer than shouting distance: 'You must stay, you stay! You not go anywhere. That is order.'

That was all I wanted to hear. No doubt he thought he was condemning me to death or at least severe illness by his decision. He did not pester me again, although I took the precaution of renewing my art work from time to time, just in case somebody else made a surprise call.

As the time passed, I began to fear that my delaying tactics had been a waste of time, for no news arrived informing me of Dad's whereabouts. In his condition I feared that he would not survive long without proper medical care and attention and I had almost resigned myself to the fact that he was dead, when one morning, almost three weeks to the day since my visit to Craigmore, Annie rushed into my room, screaming excitedly and saying there were two strange-looking Burmans who were demanding to see me. I walked warily towards them, feeling extremely suspicious, for I could not recall ever seeing a more disreputable looking couple. They were mud-caked, their clothes hung in tatters, their bodies were thin and wasted, and they looked perfectly capable of killing me for a cupful of rice. Then to my astonishment and relief, a familiar voice said: 'Hullo, Helen. Don't you recognise me? Sorry to have taken so long getting in touch.'

It was Charlie Ba Khet, the son of Colonel Ba Khet who had served in the Indian Medical Service. The other man was U Thin, the former Deputy Agricultural Officer for the area.

They explained to me that my father had been tied hand and foot and dragged away by the retreating Chinese to be beheaded at the foot of a hill about twelve miles from Craigmore. By a stroke of luck, U Thin had come across the execution squad and had successfully pleaded with them to release my father and the three Gurkha servants who had been captured at the same time. The Chinese, whose change of mind seemed as irrational as their original decision to execute an old and sick citizen of an allied country, agreed without any argument and U Thin had taken them into the jungle where Charlie Ba Khet, his father, and several prominent Burmese officials and high class Shans were striving to eke out an existence on what they could kill and snare and on wild fruit and vegetables.

Charlie said: 'Your father is not at all well, Helen, and he is worried sick about you.'

I told him it was vital to get him back to Taunggyi so that I could nurse him, but Charlie said it was not that simple. The Japanese had introduced a system of slave labour. They did not want to have large numbers of enemies or potential enemies hiding out in the countryside, at the same time they wished to avoid the problem of feeding them if the refugees came back into the town. They let it be known that anyone who wanted to enter Taunggyi in order to work as a coolie and to earn enough to buy their food, would be allowed to do so. The rate of pay would be one rupee a day. On leaving the town, Charlie explained, the labourer had to show the rupee to the guards to prove that he had earned his keep. By the end of the second day, he would have two rupees, one to buy food with, the other which he would keep so as to gain re-admittance. In this way it was hoped a regular flow of labour would result. The system sounded stupidly complicated to me, but more important, it seemed designed to keep my father away from Taunggyi. The Japanese would certainly not allow a sick man to enter the town on the pretext that he wanted to work.

Charlie, however, was a very astute man, and he understood the Japanese mentality. Orders had been issued to the guards that if anyone produced a rupee, this should be accepted as proof that he had worked the previous day. An order was an order and would be blindly obeyed. The fact that somebody who produced a rupee was clearly incapable of work was neither here nor there. He had his rupee, so he *must* have done his stint.

'As your father cannot walk we would need a *dhoolie* to carry him in, and that would need four more men, plus reliefs. If we can get hold of that number of rupees, we might be able to smuggle your father through. Have you any money, Helen?'

I shook my head. 'I haven't got a bean. I've always refused money, preferring to take goods.'

To my astonishment, Annie piped up: 'I have money, plenty.'

Wonderful Annie! Unknown to me she had been selling surplus eggs to the Japanese at an exorbitant price; three for one rupee which was more than twice their official value. No one, of course, paid much attention to that; the Japanese were as ready as anybody else to buy on the black market. All the same, Annie had been profiteering. I had always come down hard on anyone at the hospital who became involved in the thriving black market, and if I had known what she was up to would undoubtedly have stopped her. Sensibly, she had gone ahead without saying a word to me. I knew I ought to disapprove but was so delighted by the results of her misbehaviour that I could only express my gratitude.

Annie smiled her sweet smile and said: 'I have been keeping money for an emergency. Here it is.'

Charlie and U Thin pocketed the notes and promised that they would return next day with my father, providing they were able to fool the sentries.

I was unable to sleep at all that night, I was so desperately anxious to be reunited with Dad. I was up and about long before dawn. I stood on the roof of one of the outhouses and strained my eyes towards the distant forest. As daylight broke above the hills, I could just make out a small procession bearing a *dhoolie* which was moving at a snail's pace across the shrub-covered approaches to the town. My heart was in my mouth when the party stopped at the sentry post, but the soldiers seemed not in the least put out by the arrival of a sick man, they were solely concerned in making sure that everyone had the necessary one rupee for their admittance.

I rushed out to greet the procession, and was shocked to see the condition of my father; he had deteriorated so much in such a short time. As I looked down at him I could not believe that this was the same tireless man behind whom I had scrambled up in the hills when he had taught me how to shoot and fish. Apart from his physical condition, he was heartbroken at not knowing the whereabouts of my mother and sister. The scene back at the hospital was very emotional. The Gurkha servants, cook, gardener and houseboy, had been with him more than thirty years, and they fell down at his feet and wept. Loyalty, whether to a flag, a cause, or an individual, has no price; I wept unashamedly, as much for Dad as for these men to whom he could offer nothing in return.

I took his clothes off and put him to bed, while Annie washed the rags he wore. He had always been meticulous about his appearance, and he must have found it degrading to wear rags that a beggar would have tossed aside in disgust.

I fed and nursed him as best I could, but I knew that no medicine could do half as much for him as positive news of Mum and Isabel. And so when I learned on the bush telegraph, a most reliable means of communication, that a woman by the name of Rodriguez was living with other refugees in a small village outside Maymyo, I knew that somehow or other I had to get there. How it was to be done I could not imagine. In a war-stricken land, Maymyo, the summer capital of Burma, might just as well have been on the other side of the globe. With travel virtually restricted to military movements, there was no way of obtaining permission to travel there.

Before I even tried I had to find new quarters for Dad. Having got him back safely, there was no longer any need to keep open the hospital by turning patients into red-spotted Dalmatians. I solemnly informed the observer the smallpox victims had now all recovered and I was prepared to move out. The remaining patients were only too pleased to leave; no longer in need of treatment, they were desperately anxious to rejoin their families – if they could find them. U Thin volunteered to remain behind and look after Dad and we settled them in with a small group who had established themselves in one of the few bungalows that were still standing and had not been taken over by the Japanese.

Now I settled down seriously to organising my journey. On the spur of the moment, I decided to try to enlist the aid of Kodama San, a Japanese journalist attached to the Asahi Shinbun Press. I had got to know him quite well, as he had frequently visited the hospital and shown great interest in my work. He spoke fluent English, having been educated at mission schools in Japan and Canada, and was not wholeheartedly in support of the Emperor's dreams of conquest; indeed he sometimes seemed to be courting disaster by his liberal views. He was a very kind and generous young man, who had repeatedly urged me to leave Taunggyi as I was the only white woman there and he considered I was running unnecessary risks. On many occasions, he had given me his rations, and he often provided me with cigarettes and Dad with tobacco; all court-martial offences.

Journalists covering the victorious advance had considerable freedom of movement, but I wondered whether I dared ask him to get me to Maymyo. It would be inviting him to take an immense risk on my account, and I could not really see any reason why he should do so.

When I called on him and explained my plight, Kodama did not hesitate. The headquarters for war correspondents, he said, was not far from Maymyo and he would arrange to take me there in the morning. Good as his word, he arrived with a truck, gave me a white arm band similar to those worn by reporters, settled me on a settee which he had bundled into the back of the lorry, and told me to make myself as comfortable as possible for the long and tedious journey.

It was a bumpy, uncomfortable ride along cratered roads that were jam-packed with refugees who could barely drag one foot after the other; emaciated, pitiful creatures who were stumbling towards certain death. But I did not feel a jolt; I was so exhilarated at the thought of meeting Mother. We went through Meiktila; through Khaukne to Mandalay; all areas that had been devastated by the advancing Japanese. Finally we laboured up the 4000 feet climb to Maymyo, the one-time summer seat of the Government, a town not unlike India's Simla. It was well after midnight before we arrived in the hill station, once so spruce and elegant, but now a bomb-gutted shadow of its former self.

I told Kodama San that I could probably find a bed for the night in the St Joseph's Convent, but when I knocked on the door there was no reply; the nuns had all retired for the night. The wound in my leg was giving me a lot of pain, and seeing my plight, Kodama offered to take me to the Press headquarters. It was another extremely brave and generous gesture, as awk-

[80]

ward questions could well be asked by the other journalists, who were not all as favourably disposed towards the enemy as he was.

He took me to a small room no bigger than a cubicle and gestured towards the bed. 'You can sleep there.'

Tired as I was, I could not; the door had no lock and the place was filled with men I could not trust. In the darkness my fears magnified. The slightest creak signalled an intruder, and I almost screamed out in terror when I felt someone lift the mattress. Then I heard Kodama's reassuring voice. 'Do not worry. It is only me. I am tucking in a mosquito net, the place is alive with them.'

Early next morning I went out into a courtyard, washed under a tap and braided my hair, stiffened my shoulders and walked into the dining room, wondering what awaited me. The long refectory tables were lined with Japanese correspondents, none of whom could speak English; they smiled formally, then returned to their food. Some looked gaunt-eyed and tired, others fresh and relaxed. Several had towels bound tightly round their heads like turbans as an aid to concentration. I later discovered that they worked round the clock in shifts, churning out many thousands of words for the Emperor's subjects to devour over their breakfast tables.

Kodama San beckoned me to sit beside him, but unlike the others I was not served with a traditional Japanese meal; instead I was given a breakfast that would not have been out of place in a British household: hot toast and butter, a boiled egg, tea and marmalade.

Kodama did not hurry me, but as soon as I had finished he rose and took me out to a waiting Jeep – the Japanese had taken over many of these which had been abandoned by the British – and drove me along the road towards Lashio. We eventually stopped near a small village crowded with refugees who were living cheek by jowl in a ramshackle assortment of shanties made of sheets of tin, corrugated iron, palm leaves and bamboo – anything, in fact, that would provide some primitive shelter.

Women and children came out to stare at me; the sight of them turned my stomach and took away all the pleasure that my boiled egg and marmalade had given me. The children were hollow-eyed and pot-bellied, not through over-eating but from starvation. The emaciated women seemed lost and bewildered. They were all people who had not been able to fly out to India. Now they had nowhere to go, and their expressions communicated their sense of hopelessness.

I walked among them, asking if anyone knew of a Mrs Rodriguez. At last one of the women nodded, rose, and led me to a ramshackle hut dimly lit by a makeshift oil lamp. My heart soared as I entered, but it plummetted immediately when I was introduced to a dark, wizened, little old lady who said that she was Mrs Rodericks, and asked me what I wanted. Through my tears I mumbled some kind of apology. A different face, a different spelling, had dashed my hopes of my family being at last reunited. I walked back down the rutted, bullock track to where Kodama San was waiting in the Jeep, and got in without exchanging a word. The look on my face was enough to tell him that the journey had been in vain.

We drove back to Maymyo in total silence. I asked him to drop me at St Joseph's Convent, which I had last entered when I was a child of nine. I was met by Sister Emelda, who took me to see Sisters Edwards and Paul, all of whom I had met many years before in much happier times.

The classrooms were filled with refugees. I asked Sister Emelda if there happened to be any from Lashio, vaguely hoping that if there were they might have news of Mother and my sister. She said there were a few who had been stranded at the airport when the last plane flew out, and I asked to meet them. They were pitiful to see, sleeping on any vacant spot on the floor, surrounded by the few personal belongings they had managed to cling on to during their flight. As I walked among them, I met Mrs Mattie Short, who with her four children had fled from Lashio. I sat beside her and asked if she had heard or seen anything of Mrs Rodriguez and a Mr and Mrs Fuller. She

[82]

was dazed with shock, and it took her some time to answer: 'Yes, I saw them.' Mrs Rodriguez, she recalled, had had no suitcases, just a counterpane in which was wrapped a few oddments. She was carrying a small poodle under her arm. As she was being bundled on to the last plane, she had managed to exchange a few words. 'She told me she had found her Dodge car abandoned at the airstrip and had succeeded in convincing an official that it was her property. Then she had sold it to an Indian for 3000 rupees, on condition he took the dog and gave it a decent home. Having carried the poodle so far, she had been told it could not be taken aboard the aircraft.' The aircraft had eventually taken off at noon, and at two o'clock Lashio had been razed to the ground by Japanese bombers.

Mattie Short was unable to tell me any more. The poor woman was sick with worry over the safety of her own family, who had so nearly made it on the last plane out, but were now stranded in Maymyo. No more than anybody else there did they have any idea what the future might hold in store for them.

I thanked her, and thought to myself that *I* had at least got some cheering news to take back to Father. Mother and Isabel were safe!

I spent that evening talking to the nuns who told me the area around Maymyo was teeming with refugees, living in abandoned bungalows and houses. I would be far better off bringing my father up here than staying in Taunggyi where we would be a sitting target in the event of further fighting, and much more likely to attract the attention of the Japanese.

I told Kodama San of my intentions, and he again readily agreed to help, reminding me that he had repeatedly urged me to leave Taunggyi. He said he would make what arrangements he could for me to get back to Dad, and apologised for not being able to accompany me as he had to remain behind on duty.

Next morning he met me and introduced me to Ba Maung, a wiry little Burman whom he had engaged to act as my bodyguard and escort. There was, he said, nothing more he could do to guarantee my safe arrival in Taunggyi. The countryside was swarming with gangs of dacoits who thought nothing of murdering refugees and attacking anyone foolish enough to be travelling in a small group in order to steal their pitiful possessions. It was not a very cheerful prospect but there was no reason to suppose things would get any better and I was anxious to get back to my father.

The journey back was a nightmare beyond description. It had only taken me twelve hours to reach Maymyo, but it took four days of hitch-hiking to get back to Taunggyi. After thumbing a lift in three different military convoys, Ba Maung and I managed to reach Thazi, a railway junction where a scene of total chaos confronted us. The roads were strewn with the rotting, bloated corpses of humans, horses, bullocks, cats and dogs. The air was heavy with the stench of putrefying flesh, and the flies rose in black clouds when you disturbed them. Many of the dead were the victims of typhoid, cholera and dysentery; others had fallen prey to bomb blast, mortars and machine guns. What astonished me was that the Japanese made no attempt to bury or burn the bodies, something I found incomprehensible considering their obsessive fear of contagion. The more I saw of them, the more I found them a mysterious people. Amid the carnage I saw soldiers stopping to pluck a flower and savour its scent, or holding a butterfly in the palm of their hand as if to admire its delicate beauty. And then I saw the same men cold-bloodedly shoot someone in the back of the head for no apparent reason except a delight in killing.

I made my way with Ba Maung to the railway station to enquire about trains leaving for Kalaw. There was little sign of activity and I could get no sense, or even an answer, from the station master who sat cross-legged on the platform, his dog and ancient gramophone beside him, looking for all the world like the famous His Master's Voice trademark. As he sat there he listened raptly to an assortment of presumably looted records that varied from popular songs to Japanese martial music and European classics.

Neither Ba Maung nor I had tasted water for forty-eight

hours, and our tongues were cracked and swollen. When we found small deposits of water, however, we did not dare drink it as we felt it was certain to be polluted. Anyone who contracted typhoid or cholera so far from medical aid had little hope of surviving. And so we waited by the trackside, growing ever more desperate and almost crazy with thirst. Eventually Ba Maung spotted a cattle truck with an engine attached being shunted into the station. He grabbed my hand and hauled me along the rails, stumbling over the sleepers as we raced after it. Finally he managed to seize hold of a buffer, sit astride it and haul me up beside him. It took us several minutes to regain our breath before, bruised and grazed, we clambered into the foul-smelling truck and collapsed on the floor. I hoped that it was going in the general direction of Kalaw but was too exhausted to worry much about it. The important thing was that it was leaving Thazi. To have remained in that hell-hole would have meant waiting for death to release us from our plight, for we could not have survived there with disease and pestilence so rife.

Another twenty-four hours passed without our being able to quench our thirst. Although we stopped at various sidings, we never knew whether the halts would be long enough to allow us to search for water. Thirst is a curious thing, I mused. Most of our lives we take water for granted, wasting it as if there was a never-ending source. I thought of the many thousands of gallons I had sprayed on flowers, poured down drains and bath plugs, yet here I was prepared to give anything for a spoonful of the liquid. Most of the time we travelled in total silence, the effort of talking with a blackened, swollen tongue was too much. Then to our immense relief we saw we were approaching Kalaw. Daylight was just breaking and I spotted a Shan woman on the platform selling hot milk. With no other thought than to quench my thirst, I grabbed a tin mug and swallowed the entire contents. The milk was so hot that it blistered my lips and throat, adding to the excruciating pain I was already suffering.

Ba Maung and I walked into the town, happy to have got so far, but wondering how on earth we would manage the rest of the journey. Everything seemed to be moving away from Taunggyi. My leg was hurting me so much that I had to stop and rest, and so we halted at a petrol station on the main road and settled down for a long wait. Hours passed before a convoy of military lorries stopped at the pump. No one objected when we clambered into the last vehicle which was crowded with Japanese officers comfortably lounging on mattresses spread over the floor. They did not seem even to notice us; no one spoke a word or cast a glance in our direction. As far as they were concerned we did not exist. On reflection, it seems incredible that a Burmese peasant and a woman who obviously had some European blood at least should have been allowed to invade a truck reserved for Japanese officers without even a question being asked. At the time I was too tired to take in the enormity of what we were doing. Perhaps in our very apathy and indifference to the consequences lay the secret of our success.

The forty-four miles to Taunggyi took more than five hours, and we were finally dropped off at the market. Ba Maung seemed to possess the inexhaustible energy enjoyed by so many hill people, and he took the two mile walk to our destination as if it were no more than a pre-breakfast stroll. I, on the other hand, was so tired and leg-weary, I began to doubt if I would make it. I felt as if I had heavy lead weights shackled to my ankles, and it was as much as I could do to haul one foot after the other as far as the bungalow to which Dad had been moved.

Waiting to greet me was the McIntyre family – which had turned up in Taunggyi since our departure – U Thin and several others who had formed a small and friendly community. Dad was bursting to hear my news, but I had to have a drink of water first. The temptation was to drink the well dry, but I resisted, knowing how dangerous it could be. The water was better than the finest champagne, even so the effort of talking was extremely painful. But the look of delight on Dad's face on hearing that Mum and Isabel were safe, made the whole terrible journey worthwhile.

Two nights later as we sat around talking, U Thin said that he had discovered Ba Maung was a medium. He had asked him to conduct a seance in the hope of getting some news about his wife and two daughters who had disappeared during the evacuation. Mr McIntyre was more than willing to join in, as he had lost all trace of his brother who was a doctor. At that time, I was extremely sceptical about people who claimed to possess the gift of being able to contact the spirit world; in any event, I found that my religion gave me all the strength and confidence I needed to carry on without resorting to any such quackery.

It occurred to me, however, that I was being extremely selfish; knowing my own mother and sister were safe I had forgotten to what desperate lengths people still in doubt would go so as to obtain some news about lost loved ones. So I agreed to fall in with the wishes of the others; if further news emerged about my mother and sister, all well and good; if, as I felt certain would prove to be the case, it was a waste of time, I had lost nothing. Dad, however, would have no part of it. He stoutly refused even to remain in the room 'listening to a load of mumbo jumbo'.

It was an eerie experience. We squatted in a small circle in the bombed-out shell of a room with Ba Maung in the middle, and asked our questions through U Thin. The little hillman seemed to go into a trance, and when U Thin asked him the whereabouts of his family he replied in a voice totally different to his own. They had gone north, he intoned, on water; they were among *phongyis* (priests) and were perfectly safe. Mr McIntyre then asked about his brother Norman. The strange voice that had invaded Ba Maung became almost a whisper. 'I see dark water and deep.' He would say no more, despite Mr McIntyre's repeated appeals.

When my turn came, I asked about my mother and sister. The voice that emerged from Ba Maung's lips was harsh and

[87]

angry. 'You are an unbeliever. Why do you ask this?'

I was so taken aback that I hardly knew what to say. I blurted out what I actually felt. 'That is true. I am. But I asked with respect, and truthfully I would like to know where they are.'

There was a long pause, and the silence in the room was almost tangible before a child's voice replied: 'They are north and moving far south in another country.'

I lost interest; I had learned nothing new. I knew that Mother and Isabel had flown to India, and I was not too impressed with what he had told the others.

I only mention the incident, because many years later I met U Thin in India and enquired about his family. He said he had found them safe and being well cared for by priests in a remote village. Mr McIntyre also discovered that Ba Maung's strange message had been sadly true; Norman had been drowned while trying to cross a monsoon-swollen river.

*   *   *

It took me several weeks to recover from the rigours of the trip, but as soon as I felt fit enough to travel I told Father that the time had come for us to make our way to Maymyo. Kodama San was now back in Taunggyi and I again sought his help. Once more he unhesitatingly gave it. Somehow or other he managed to borrow a 15-cwt. truck, no mean achievement in a town where transport was precious and closely guarded. By the time I had lifted Dad and his bed into the back, along with our few personal belongings; and the McIntyres, with their four children, two dogs, a cockatoo, and some hens and ducks had boarded, the truck was sagging on its springs.

I pleaded with Annie to join us, but she shook her head. Her drunken Madrassi husband, who had vanished when Taunggyi was first bombed, had turned up some weeks previously like the bad penny he was. He was drunk when he arrived, and he stayed in that condition, making himself such a nuisance that I was eventually forced to ban him from entering the house and compound. Incredibly, Annie, who had been as upset as I was at his unexpected reappearance, refused to abandon him. 'Madam, much as I love you, I feel my loyalty is here.'

I knew there was no point in arguing, although I felt sad for her, and bitter that so worthless a man should exact such a sacrifice. I gave her what money I could spare, along with a few pots and pans and crockery, and we embraced. As we drove off she stood alone, weeping and waving goodbye. We both knew how little chance there was that we would ever meet again. Sleeping off his hangover in one of the sheds was the man she had refused to leave. He neither knew nor cared what she had given up for him.

The roads were still choked with an endless procession of refugees, and it seemed an eternity before we reached Shwe Naung, just twelve miles down the hill. There we unloaded, camped out in the goods terminal and waited patiently for a train to carry us on the next stage of our long journey. After a lot of bullying and coaxing, the station master allocated us two trucks and warned us that he could not say how long it would take, or even guarantee that it would arrive at our destination. After numerous postponements, the ancient train chugged out of the station and headed for Kalaw, clinking and clanking as if it would fall apart with every thrust of the pistons. There was another appalling delay at Kalaw before the wheezy old engine gave a toot and began its long descent to the plains.

It was June, and the heat was unbearable; it hit you as if a furnace door had been opened a few feet away from you, a sure sign that the monsoon was not far off. My head pounded and my eyes kept losing focus, but there was no escape from the relentless pressure. Water was scarce and had to be carefully rationed; just enough was issued to moisten the throat and ease the pain of parched lips. Our meals, mainly rice, were cooked over hastily built fires between the railway sleepers. Washing was a rare luxury and we were coated with dust which the perspiration dried on our skin until our faces resembled clay masks. When we needed to go to the toilet we had to venture into the jungle that lined the track, taking our lives in our hands, for bands of marauders still roamed at large, looting whatever they could and lying in wait for someone to kill and rob.

After five and a half days we pulled into Mandalay. The once beautiful city was in ruins. Non-stop air attacks had reduced many of its splendid buildings to rubble, while the mainly timber-built native quarters had been devastated by incendiaries.

We were still about forty miles from our destination, and at the rate we were travelling it would take us another two days at least. My father and the children were finding the torment of the journey even more intolerable than I was. I threw discretion to the wind, had a whip round for money, and went in search of a taxi. It was a forlorn hope, but worth a try.

I did not recognise the Mandalay I had known in my teens. The magnificent Palace of the Kings, renamed Fort Dufferin by the British and the scene of the most splendid durbar in 1940, seemed intact but was teeming with Japanese soldiers. The streets, once crowded with saffron-robed monks begging for food and alms, were empty; the shops, where for centuries craftsmen had produced gold and silver umbrellas, lay deserted and silent. The famous pagoda where thousands of pilgrims from all over the country journeyed to worship the Buddha enthroned below a gold-beamed ceiling, was empty except for a handful of downcast and preoccupied monks.

I walked through street after street, once bustling with people and creaking bullock carts, now strangely mute, before I stumbled upon a battered T-Ford whose owner agreed to take the lot of us to Maymyo for forty rupees. It was far more than we could afford, but the alternative was to stick with the train, and I was not at all confident that if we did so, the whole party would arrive alive at its destination.

As the car set off, it resembled a scene from some old Hollywood comedy. On the roof the hens were squawking, the ducks quacking, the dogs barking their heads off. Inside we were packed tighter than baked beans. The children were not making things any easier by bawling their indignation at the discomfort. We might have qualified for the Guinness Book of Records, if anyone at that time had seen any special merit in cramming more people than would seem humanly possible into a small car. It was excruciatingly uncomfortable, but at least the car had an engine and wheels.

We arrived in Maymyo in the middle of an air raid, and made our way to the address Kodama San had given me in Forest Road. It proved to be a pleasant bungalow, bare of all furniture, but with a lovely and still well-kept garden.

I managed to settle Dad in one of the rooms, and to lock the livestock in an outhouse, before collapsing. I felt like a sailor who has been too long at sea, my legs could still feel the motion of the train and the ramshackle taxi, and they rebelled at the thought of any further walking. Our taxi driver was so concerned about my condition that he helped carry most of our belongings into the house, and then refused a tip.

When my legs decided to rejoin my body, I prepared a rough and ready meal from the provisions Kodama San had delivered to the house, but the thought of eating myself was too much for my queasy stomach. Instead I flopped down on the floor and went to sleep.

Next morning I took stock of the situation. The first thing that I decided was that I could not survive without some means of transport in order to go shopping. I walked into town and scoured those few shops that were still open. At last I found an old upright cycle which I bought for fifty rupees.

Our new-found home turned out to be a very temporary haven. After a week, Kodama San arrived at the door and announced that we were moving to Joyville, a curiously named bungalow which had been previously owned by a Mr Jellicoe. It was a handsome house, but once again deprived of all furniture. I glanced around the rooms and at once decided that it could be made reasonably comfortable if I could only lay my hands on a few beds, chairs and tables. These might be difficult to find, but an even more intractable problem was how to get them to our house once I had found them. The solution came in a most unexpected manner.

I was walking through the nearby forest one morning, hoping to find someone selling fruit and vegetables, when I met an old man collecting firewood and bundling it on to an ancient cart. I asked him if I could hire it, and he readily agreed to rent it out when he had finished with it, at the lordly sum of two rupees a day. And so throughout the next week I carried out a house-to-house collection service, picking up a chair here, a table there, odd bits of crockery and kitchen utensils, until Joyville slowly began to look more like a home. Having been a hill retreat for the well-off, and the summer seat of the government, there proved to be no shortage of furniture. Many of the inhabitants had simply locked their doors and fled; some of their homes had been looted, but those which had not looked as if their owners had merely gone away for the weekend.

I felt no particular qualms about 'borrowing' things from their houses – our need, after all, was desperate and the stuff would otherwise have been lying idle. When I came across an abandoned piano, however, I felt that this was going a bit too far. Could I really reconcile it with my conscience to requisition such an expensive and inessential item? Kodama San soon quashed my doubts, however; airily assuring me that it was quite all right. He even helped me load it on to the cart.

I quickly settled down and began to experience my first taste of peace and tranquillity since the Japanese had invaded Burma.

As the weeks passed, word got around that I was a qualified nurse. Soon patients from the town and nearby villages began turning up at the house for treatment. The villagers apologised for not having any money and therefore not being able to pay for their treatment, but they offered instead eggs, small amounts of rice and the odd cup of flour. That suited me down to the ground. If they had been able to pay I would only have spent the money on food, and would probably have had to pay on the black market prices far higher than those which I could have brought myself to charge the patients. Soon my practice extended until I became an unofficial district nurse, paying regular visits to outlying villages and settlements. I was kept hard at it from morning till night, treating cases of malaria, dysentery, open sores brought about by malnutrition, shrapnel wounds, and other injuries. On top of that, I still had to tend our own growing community who seemed to be taken ill with depressing regularity.

Laying my hands on medicines and drugs was my main problem. Some of the old native women gave me centuries-old remedies, which entailed the use of herbs, kernels of nuts, and roots, and in certain cases these proved strikingly effective. There were always some ailments, however, that needed modern drugs to treat them and to find anything appropriate proved exceedingly difficult. Occasionally I managed to obtain a small supply of smuggled drugs from an army veterinary surgeon, but the stock he gave me never lasted very long. It was an extraordinary piece of luck that even this limited supply was available to me. What happened was that one of my dogs whelped. As the vet was passing by one day on horseback, he stopped to admire the litter and asked me if I would sell him one. Sell? I was only too glad to give him one! It meant one less mouth to feed. But he felt he had to repay me in some way, and so began to drop in small quantities of medicine, pills, and drugs. He became something of a local character, for whenever he rode through the streets the dog was always perched on the pommel of his saddle.

Without the proper medical equipment and material, I quickly discovered the truth of the old axiom that necessity is the mother of invention. One day I was cycling back from a confinement when a small Mohammedan girl, aged about six, was knocked down in the market place by a Japanese lorry. The tiny figure was tossed over the bonnet high into the air, but the driver did not even bother to stop. I dismounted and rushed to her side; I did not have to make too detailed an examination to see that her arm was badly broken in two places.

Her father was frantic and pleaded with me to do something about it. I knew what had to be done well enough, but did not have the means of doing it. I could reset the bones, but I had no plaster of paris in which to encase her arm. Then I happened to spot a large ant hill.

'Get me some *dhoti* cloth,' I demanded, and the near-demented father scuttled off like a startled rabbit. Then I despatched several of the onlookers to scoop out handfuls of the very fine dust from the ant hill. I lay the child down by the roadside, reset her shattered arm, then mixed the dust with some water until it was the consistency of thick porridge. Having done that, I tore the *dhoti* cloth into long strips and applied it to her arm along with the improvised plaster. I waited until it had dried cement-hard, which did not take long in the searing heat, and instructed the waiting father to curb his curiosity and leave the 'plaster' on for at least six weeks. Then he could take a knife and carefully cut through it, making sure not to damage the flesh. He thanked me profusely, picked up the child and headed for the nearby jungle.

I remounted my cycle and rode home, very apprehensive about my impromptu operation. I had done my best, but I could not help thinking that the child might be crippled for life in spite of my efforts. My ant hill plaster could set up an infection; the father might be impatient and remove it prematurely; the bones might not have set properly; the plaster might crumble back into the dust it had once been long before the scheduled time. . . . The number of things that could go wrong seemed endless. I could only pray for her recovery, though it did not seem likely that I would ever find out what happened. In the conditions which ruled in Burma then, I thought I would never see father or child again. I was to be proved very wrong.

I was perfectly content tending the sick, but I realised I could not carry on indefinitely. It was becoming increasingly hard to obtain the basic necessities of life. The little that my patients were able to give me decreased as they became more and more in need themselves. The black market flourished and prices rose alarmingly. If you wanted to purchase anything of any value, you needed to carry around a haversack filled with the almost worthless Japanese currency. Even that would not get you very far. Gradually, I had to sell what little jewellery I had been able to hang on to, and when that had gone I began selling anything that remained which could be worth a few rupees: our mosquito nets, linen, the hard won furniture. . . . At the rate I was emptying Joyville, it would soon be as barren as the day I arrived. The only thing that was not scarce was the demand on my time and nursing skill. As conditions worsened, the 'panel' of patients increased alarmingly in size, while the food I received in return seemed to get less and less. Unless I took some decisive action, I would be too weak from malnutrition to resist disease myself, and all those who depended on me would be left to fend for themselves.

During my rounds I was given a lot of advice and kept up to date with the local news. One day, when I was telling a patient how hard I found it to make ends meet, she said: 'Why not try your luck in Rangoon? There's a lot of money to be made there.' Rangoon was a long way from Maymyo, but the McIntyres offered to look after Dad and the animals, and I knew he could not be in better hands. Anyway, I did not plan to stay away long; if Rangoon did indeed prove as satisfactory as my patient suggested then I would have to try to think up some way of getting my father there as well.

It was around this time that I received a letter from my mother. She had obviously had some doubts about it ever reaching me, as the enveloped was addressed in the most odd manner:

Prisoner of War Post for Prisoners
Service de Prisonniers de Guerre
Miss H. Rodriguez (Matron) Civil Hospital Taunggyi
Southern Shan States
Burma.

British Prisoner of War c/o Japanese Red Cross Tokyo.

I still feel it was something of a miracle that this letter should somehow have crossed the frontier between two warring nations and reached me safely. When it at last caught up with me, Taunggyi had been crossed through in red ink and Maymyo substituted, and it was covered with indecipherable postmarks.

The letter (still a treasured possession) gave Mother's address as the Government Isolation Hospital, Bangalore, India:

'My dearest Helen,
If you are at our dear home I know you will be at your hospital doing your good work for the sick. I have worried over you and pray God will keep you safe. Some say you are still in Taunggyi. I do not know why you did not leave with me, dear, but the wounded were in your heart. I know no harm will come to you when you have given your love and care for the sick, my dear one. I hope you will get my letters, they will cheer you up. You have Dad to care for, dear, and one day we will all be together again. I often wish with all my heart that I had stayed behind with you. I was pushed on to that lorry and you said you would follow up. I waited for hours in vain. Now all I pray for is that you are safe and well and we will meet again.
Love, Mums.'

I wept as I read her words. I was heartened to have at last heard from her, yet at the same time I was chilled. The writing was scrawled and almost unintelligible. Mum had always had such a beautiful hand, yet these sentences were disjointed and difficult to read. I realised she had gone through hell, and that the marks of it were plain to see.

Father could not control a flood of tears, but at least they were of relief. The letter put him in a much happier frame of

[96]

mind, so that I had no qualms about leaving him in order to try to earn some money in Rangoon. If I failed, I had little doubt that our chances of seeing the war through would be very slim indeed.

Chapter 5

I was resigned to the fact that travel in wartime Burma was a test of endurance and the trip to Rangoon confirmed it with a vengeance. I made the journey in a freight train wagon loaded with garlic and ginger, and I arrived days later feeling and smelling like a pickled onion. Rangoon, which I knew well and loved so much, bore the scars of the Japanese air raids, but despite the fact that a vast number of its population had fled, it was still a bustling port, supplying the Japanese with much of their war material. It was not exactly business as usual, but the city was gradually getting back on its feet.

The McIntyres had given me the address of an old Shan friend in Rangoon, and she very kindly offered to put me up until I found work and quarters of my own. My first call early next morning was to the Diocesan Girls' School, which had been turned into an emergency hospital. There to my immense relief and surprise I found I knew the Civil Surgeon in charge. Without hesitation I asked him if he would employ me.

'Certainly, Helen, I'd be delighted to, but only on one condition. You must change your name, and wear Burmese clothes.'

'Don't bother to say any more,' I retorted. 'I will not change my name, nor will I alter my dress. You must take me as I am or not at all.'

'It's for your own safety,' he insisted. 'A white woman here is always in danger, whereas the Japanese are trying desperately hard to convince the Burmese they are friends.'

It would have been simple to agree to his suggestion, but I could not bring myself to do it. I felt that it would be tantamount to conceding victory to the Japs. To do so would be to make a mockery of what I, Mum and Dad had endured; still worse, to act in this way for cash would have been a piece of treachery.

No doubt I was being melodramatic and had got things thoroughly out of proportion, but it seemed to me that if I gave way the doctor would have been entitled to offer me thirty pieces of silver as wages.

He could see from my determined expression that I was adamant, and so he dropped the subject. 'There is somebody upstairs who would love to see you,' he said. 'Sister Daw Khin Kyi.'

I was delighted at the unexpected news. It was wonderful to meet an old friend after so many years; we had nursed together in happier times in Rangoon and become close friends. In her room she confided to me that she had met a patient in a private ward, and had become extremely fond of him. They proposed to marry shortly. His name was General Aung San, the Burman whom the Japanese had made a Major-General and Commander-in-Chief of their puppet Burma National Army. He had been anti-British before the war and secretary of the Nationalist Minority Group. In 1940, when his organization had been proscribed, he and some of the other members had managed to flee to Japan. There he had been trained in an officers' school and indoctrinated with the belief that Japan would soon drive the British out of Burma and bring freedom to its people. He returned to his homeland with the Japanese invasion forces, and helped organise a fifth column.

I was not over-impressed with Khin Kyi's choice, and was only half-hearted in my congratulations. But of course I did not want to hurt her feelings and was filled with excitement when she went on to say that she had been offered a post at the hospital for The Little Sisters of the Poor in Kandawelay. Now she would not be taking it up. Why should I not apply to fill her place? I needed no encouragement and was on my way to the hospital without even stopping for the proffered meal – some-

[99]

thing which half an hour earlier I would have given my right arm for.

(Here I will digress. In fairness to General Aung San, I must say that I met him a number of times and grew to like him. He was not a devious intriguer but a man who deeply loved his country and wanted to see it independent. He quickly discovered that the independence the Japanese spoke of bore no relation to what he wanted; he had simply exchanged one master for a far more tyrannical one. As time passed he became more and more disillusioned. In the end he offered his services and that of his army to the British. Some of the more died-in-the-wool members of the old regime were outraged at the proposal and wanted it turn down out of hand, but Mountbatten and Slim had no doubt at all that we should accept his services. They never had cause to regret their decision. Aung San fought under General Slim, who was most impressed with him, finding him a genuine patriot. His reward for his unswerving dedication to Burmese independence was death; he and several ministers of the first independent government were assassinated by supporters of U Saw who burst into the Executive Council Room in July 1947 and opened fire on the ministers with machine guns. U Saw was later hanged for his role in the plot.)

The doctor in charge at the hospital was Dr Suzuki, who had enjoyed a lucrative practice in peacetime Rangoon. He was one of the large number of Japanese residents who had lived in the port, and had been regarded with amused tolerance by the British. They were mainly doctors, dentists and photographers, who were often sickeningly obsequious in their desire to please the Europeans. The photographers snapped the children of the army wives, and photographed the garrison when it carried out parades and manoeuvres. The dentists drilled, filled and extracted teeth and gently pumped their patients for information. The doctors did the same. It never occurred to anyone that these helpful, harmless technicians had been recruited by the Japanese Intelligence Service to spy on the people they served and report all they found out to Tokyo. So, when the Japs did invade, the strength of the army and the easiest routes into Burma were well known to them.

My interview with Dr Suzuki was brief and to the point: the job was mine, providing I had the attributes of the three wise monkeys – I was to hear nothing, see nothing, and keep my mouth shut. If I was interested I would be placed in charge of the private out-patients department. The salary was seventy-five rupees a month. I readily agreed to the conditions, which I did not foresee causing me any inconvenience; there was no one I could confide in, even if I had wanted to.

The work was hard, but I had no complaints; the pay was exceptionally good in a city where a lot of people were little better off than slaves. I soon discovered that if the Japanese wanted anything done they recruited people in a most arbitrary fashion, without giving the slightest thought as to whether or not the labourer was worthy of his hire, or the hire was an adequate reward for the labour.

Doctor Suzuki was a pleasant enough man, an extremely able doctor and, incidentally, Governor of the city, but he was mainly interested in feathering his own nest. The hospital was run very much on a hit-and-miss basis; if a patient got fed he was lucky. My room had once been a nun's cell, small and so narrow that it could only just accommodate a bed. Being windowless, it was as hot as a baker's oven. The only thing remaining in the hospital to remind anyone that it had once been a Christian institution was the row of decapitated religious statues which lay strewn around the courtyard, like victims of some hideous massacre. The beautiful chapel had been desecrated and the altar vandalised.

Dr Suzuki insisted on his personal patients paying him in British money. Although an ardent supporter of his masters, he had little faith in the Japanese currency. The private fees he received went straight into his pocket; unfortunately for him, they often came straight out again. He had two, not one, Achilles heels: a weakness for hard drink, and an infatuation with his Karen mistress. But he had no head for strong drink, and she did not let her heart rule hers. When she put him to bed at night she emptied his pockets of the fees he had earned; when he woke up he was too fuddled to remember, or too much in thrall to his mistress to make any protest.

Much of his income came from rich out-patients, many of whom were women who observed strict purdah. This meant that no man other than the husband should see them unveiled, let alone examine the most secret parts of their anatomy. It was an out-moded but jealously guarded custom for which I had no tolerance, but I grew to see the advantages of it, for it turned out to be a gold mine for me. As I grew to know the women better, many confided in me that they had grave misgivings about being examined by a man. They would much prefer to be treated by me at their homes. Surprisingly, Dr Suzuki raised no objections when I asked for his permission; he had more patients than he could personally handle, and as long as his revenue did not suffer unduly, was quite content for me to go ahead. He went even further and allowed me to use his private car for my calls. After two months of this system, I was earning so much that I was repaying him the seventy-five rupees I received as wages in return for the petrol I used.

I did, however, relax the principle which I had defended with such arrogance during my visit to the hospital in the Diocesan Girls' School. When people in the street saw that I was a European I found that they often abused me. I never felt in real danger but it was unpleasant and emotionally exhausting. After a time I began to wear a sari. At first I was rather shamefaced about it, but soon I found that it was no great sacrifice; on the contrary, it proved an extremely comfortable and sensible dress for the hot climate. I quickly appreciated why it was the traditional garb among Indian women and regretted that I had not adopted it years before.

Soon I was earning as much as two thousand rupees a month, a small fortune at the time, and as my little nest egg mounted I began to make plans for my return to Maymyo. I started buying essentials for Dad; but prices were so astronomical that my money began to disappear at an alarming rate. A pair of flannel trousers cost me several hundred rupees, a shirt forty-five, a vest about the same amount. What I paid for a pair of shoes would in peacetime have shod a platoon of soldiers. A second-hand umbrella – a vital possession in Burma, whether it was to keep off the rain or the sun – cost an exorbitant two hundred and fifty rupees. So, although I was earning a lot of money, I was going through it like a rake through his inheritance. I appreciated the wisdom of Dr Suzuki insisting on being paid in British money. The more I earned the more I spent on items which I knew were unobtainable in Maymyo; not luxuries but little things that in normal times I took for granted. My hard-won savings gone, I had to hang on and earn more. I became a magpie and began to hoard feverishly: reels of cotton, needles, strips of elastic, cards of buttons. Several shops openly sold clothing which had been abandoned by the British army when it withdrew from Rangoon, and I purchased quite a lot of odds and ends. What leisure time I had was invariably spent scouring the bazaars for things which had long since vanished in Maymyo.

Then unexpectedly, I was introduced to a fresh and very fertile source of funds. One day I walked into the out-patients department and saw Dr Suzuki engrossed in conversation with a high-ranking Japanese officer. I could tell from the glances cast in my direction that I was the subject of their discussion. For a moment I feared that the authorities were taking an undesirable interest in my existence, but quickly dismissed the idea. What harm was I possibly doing to the Japanese?

Dr Suzuki took me aside and quietly asked me if I would be prepared to work in an operating theatre some distance from the hospital. The condition would be that I did not mention to anyone anything that I saw or heard there. As that was already a condition of my employment I had no difficulty in agreeing.

Three days later I was summoned to his office. A soldier blindfolded me and bundled me into a waiting car, then drove me to a hospital which had been set up for VIP's and senior officers on the Prome Road. I was baffled by all this futile mystery. I already knew of the existence of the hospital which was openly talked about in The Little Sisters of the Poor (and of the rich, too, as I had now discovered!). As for the blindfold, it was a waste of time; I knew Rangoon intimately, having trudged through its streets hour after hour in search of things to buy. At no point did I have any doubt which way the car was going.

When I arrived at the hospital the blindfold was removed and I was led into a large, very modern operating theatre which boasted the finest equipment and was scrupulously clean. I was handed a spotless sterilised gown, cap, mask, slippers and gloves, and told I was needed to assist at a major operation. For some reason everyone in the theatre spoke German, which as I could not speak a word of the language, made it difficult for me to follow the surgeon's instructions. But I coped, and when the operation was finished and I was scrubbing down I was taken aside and handed an envelope containing a hundred rupees. Then I was again blindfolded, put in the car and driven back to my quarters. I never discovered who the patient was, or the reason for the ludicrous secrecy; nor did I find out why the operating team spoke German. But I made further trips to the hospital and got the same fee on each occasion. It all helped to pay for more buttons or bandages.

During my visits to the bazaars I was puzzled by the number of nuns' habits which were on sale. It seemed that no one ever bought them, yet they were always conspicuously displayed. That was a mystery I *was* allowed to solve. I made discreet enquiries among my colleagues and found out that the nuns from The Little Sisters of the Poor had all been rounded up before I arrived and herded into quarters in a squalid part of Rangoon, where they lived in solitary confinement, not being able to go out since they had no clothes to wear. I assume that displaying their religious habits in public was just another way by which the Japanese sought to humiliate them. My nest egg, which I counted with such pride and pleasure each evening, now suffered a sad blow. I spent several hundred rupees buying all the habits I could lay my hands on. The nuns were overjoyed when I turned up in Dr Suzuki's car which was packed to the roof with their own clothes. I only hope they were left in peace to wear them.

I had little time to find out because I was growing tired of Rangoon and anxious to rejoin my father. I pestered Dr Suzuki for permission to return to Maymyo, until eventually and reluctantly he gave his consent, with the stern warning that if I did not return I would be arrested. I made the journey up country without too much difficulty. Dad was delighted to see me, and tried all his persuasive powers to get me to stay. I dearly wanted to, but I had more sense than to upset Dr Suzuki, and so returned to the hospital.

It was at this stage that I met the dashing, or so he thought, colonel. He was a tall, thin, spare man with a straggling goatee beard, always immaculately dressed in a stiff well-starched uniform. After I had seen him a few times he began to take more than a passing interest in me. I rejected his advances. Dr Suzuki warned me that I should be a little more accommodating, as he was a powerful man in Rangoon and I would be wise not to upset him. It was sensible advice; unfortunately the colonel did not appeal to me in the least. I had no desire to go for moonlight rides in a motor car with any Japanese officer, and this one less than most. I told him so in no uncertain manner. But the colonel was not easily dissuaded and continued his advances with relentless zeal. When words failed him he resorted to gifts, which I also refused.

He was entitled to full marks for persistence. One morning a car arrived at the hospital, and an enormous dressing table with an ornate, gilt, circular mirror was carried up to my room by two perspiring soldiers. 'Get that thing out of here,' I bellowed angrily, but they ignored me, saying it was a gift from the colonel, and it was more than their lives were worth to return it. Even if I had wanted the ridiculous object and had been disposed to accept his presents, however, I could hardly have done so. The cell in which I was living was small enough as it was; when the dressing table was moved in there was no room to move. I dug in my heels, and back it went.

The colonel switched his tactics; if I was not to be softened by midnight car trips or lavish presents, then he would resort to the written word. He began to send me love letters which I used to get translated, if only out of curiosity. They were touching in their inadequacy; the colonel was so wooden and formal that he was clearly ill at ease when putting his thoughts on paper. One letter began: 'My Helen, Your eyes look like the reflection of the Maymyo lakes' – well-intentioned, no doubt, but hardly a phrase calculated to win me over. Large and muddy, perhaps he meant? Or just watery? I had no pretensions to beauty but felt I deserved better than that. I could see that I was not going to get anywhere with polite rebuffs, so one afternoon I confronted him and said: 'Colonel, you are a very important man, and you must know full well that you have orders not to fraternise with us. I am not disobeying the law, so why should you?'

He stood there, rattled his sword menacingly in its scabbard, and warned me to watch my step. But it worked. There were no more dressing tables, and thankfully no more letters. I do not know whether my words had hit home, but I suppose they must have. He continued to be extremely friendly and charming, though, so it did not seem that he bore me any grudge for my temerity. I must confess that I was not above taking advantage of his friendship from time to time, and do not remember feeling even a twinge of conscience. I managed to persuade him to send extra rations to Dad, and an occasional supply of drugs, and from time to time he allowed me to visit Maymyo. I was the only female on the crowded troop trains, and it said a lot for his reputation that I was not once molested.

Even so, Dr Suzuki never failed to remind me that *he* was my employer, and despite the colonel's position of authority he insisted that I could not remain in Maymyo. 'The consequence will be very serious if you disobey,' he solemnly warned me. He had no need to go on about it. He was, after all, the Governor, and at first I had no intention of putting his threat to the test.

As time passed, however, I began to pluck up my courage to take a calculated risk. If I did not take some decisive step, I would be stuck in Rangoon for the duration of the war. I gambled on my belief that Dr Suzuki was basically quite well disposed towards me, and that though he would huff and puff in his efforts to get me back, he would stop short of having me arrested. On my next trip to Maymyo I decided to defy him. I received two irate letters ordering me to report back without delay, but I ignored them. I was just beginning to think that I had got away with it when I was served with a notice to report to the police station in Maymyo. There I was told that, as I had flagrantly disobeyed orders, I would be required to work as a 'maid' in the officers mess. I knew exactly what that entailed; I had heard from other young women who had been recruited for this unsavoury employment. I flew into a furious rage and said that I was a nurse employed to treat the sick. I had no intention of ending up as a forces' comfort! My rage had no visible effect on the police, but a hefty bribe had better results. I was let off with a stern warning and thus avoided incarceration in what would have been to all intents and purposes a Japanese brothel.

Some time around December, Dad and I received orders that we must leave Joyville and move to a house on the Mandalay-Lashio Road, which had been requisitioned by the army. The McIntyres had received their marching orders some time before. There was no question of our protesting, so Dad and I gathered together our few possessions and went into this big, gloomy house which echoed with loneliness, along with the two dogs, Cocky the cockatoo, bequeathed to me by the Mcintyres, and a couple of rather bedraggled ducks. As the days slid by, more people who had been directed to the area began moving to the outlying districts as rumours persisted that the British were about to drop parachutists. As the people moved to relative safety, so the number of my patients began to dwindle. The price of food soared like a thermometer in a heat wave, and the money I had accumulated in Rangoon was quickly spent.

On Christmas Eve I was terribly depressed. There seemed nothing to feel festive about. Apart from the two ducks, there was not a scrap of food in the house, and I was completely out of that commodity essential in the tropics – salt. It is only when you are without salt that you realise its importance. In hot climates its absence can mean death. As I banged and shook the empty cannister, I thought to myself, no wonder the word salary derives from the Latin 'sal' for salt, and that 'worthy of his salt' is the ultimate accolade!

Among the few families who had not moved out were the Haskinses: father, mother and two boys. Mr Haskins was bed-ridden and his wife was having a far worse time of it than I was. Even so she found time to spare us a thought, and sent round the two boys to wish Dad and I a Merry Christmas. They were aged fourteen and sixteen, but when they arrived on the doorstep I could not have guessed their age, they were so thin and emaciated. I felt sorry for them and said: 'If you can catch the two ducks you can take them home to your mother.' I have never seen two lads move more quickly; the ducks never had a chance.

As they scuttled off, the quacking birds hanging from their hands, I reflected that perhaps I had been a trifle over-generous. It would have been more prudent to have hung on to at least one of the birds. But it was no good regretting my impetuosity. I walked round the dust-filled garden wondering where I could get hold of some food. Then I saw a man cycling towards the house with several bundles hanging from his crossbar and handlebars. It was only when he came through the gate and salaamed that I recognised him as the father of the little girl whose broken arm I had reset. He said he had been looking everywhere for me as he wished to tell me that she had made a complete recovery, and was able to use her hand as well as ever. It was only recently that someone had told him of my whereabouts, and as a token of his gratitude he had brought me a little food for the Christian festival. A little! I broke down and sobbed as he tipped the contents of the bundles on to the table. Out tumbled a whole leg of mutton, vegetables, tins of cooking oil, bags of flour, dhal, rice, some spices and, as if he had read my thoughts, salt. He waved aside my thanks, mounted his cycle and rode away.

I never saw him again. It was chastening to know that our survival had depended on a roadside ant hill. I was glad for the sake of the little girl that her arm had healed so well, glad too that my ham-handed doctoring had proved so effective, but I must confess that at that moment I was gladdest of all to know that we would have a square meal on Christmas Day. The next day we sat down to a real Christmas dinner. Even the dogs had generous helpings.

A few days later, at the beginning of January, we suffered our first air raid from British aircraft. It was shortly after 1 a.m. – I can pinpoint the time, but not the day, for I had no calendar or newspaper to remind me – when the sky was filled with the ominous, deep throb of aircraft engines. Suddenly the whole area was illuminated, as if daylight had arrived prematurely. I ran out and stood on the porch, entranced, watching the parachute flares slowly descending. I thought to myself: how pretty they look! Then a series of violent explosions rocked the town, and I realised the flares were markers for the bombers. I managed to get Dad under the table before I heard a terrible whistling noise, followed by an enormous bang, the blast of which hurled me right across the room. Several more explosions followed, but miraculously the house remained standing. When I went out to see what damage there was, I discovered one bomb had fallen straight down the well only twenty yards away, but had failed to explode.

As the raid continued, I became conscious of a different sound; the incessant rumble of wheels and the creak of axles. When I looked out on the road running past the house, I saw that it was jammed with people fleeing from the town, carrying their belongings in every conceivable form of transport: bullock carts, hand carts, traps, tongas, even perambulators. They had no idea where they were going, but, like me, they knew full well the raid would be the forerunner of many more.

Sleep was impossible that night, and in the morning I made Dad his breakfast, then told him to pack a few things while I went down to the Clergy House to ask Father Keo if he would take him in until I had found somewhere less dangerous to live. Father Keo was delighted to help, so I borrowed a hand cart and trundled Dad, his belongings, Cocky, and the two dogs along to the Clergy House. Then I cycled over to the railway quarters, where I knew several families were still living, to find out what plans they had made for evacuation. Mr Garnet D'Cruz, who had been appointed their spokesman, said they had been promised shelter in a zinc-roofed school building in Barabattia village, about six miles away. He was sure there was room for two more. I returned home, loaded as much as I could on to my cycle and returned to the railway quarters, where I was told I could remain until we departed for Barabattia.

About six o'clock next morning I was taking some washing off the line when I heard the familiar and dreaded roar of engines. People emerged from their rooms and began to run towards the large L-shaped slit trench, yelling for me to follow. I was about to do so when from out of the corner of my eye I saw Cocky tearing around in a panic and squawking his head off. I chased after him, intending to take him to the shelter, but he kept eluding my outstretched hands and managed to nip under the table. I crawled after him, whispering comforting phrases, and had just grabbed him by the leg when the first bomb fell. The house rocked on its foundations, and lumps of brick and mortar showered down on to the top of the table. Mercifully it was solid enough to resist the blows. With Cocky under my arm I ran out into the compound, aware of an awesome silence that had descended. Not a voice could be heard through the dust and smoke. I went over to the trench and looked down; all thirteen of the occupants were dead. There was not a mark on any of them, although their faces had a bluish tinge. The blast from the bomb had collapsed their lungs.

There was no time to give them a proper funeral, so those of us who had escaped filled in the trench. It was only too obvious that it would be senseless to delay our departure a moment longer than was necessary. I again borrowed a cart, collected Dad, piled what I could on to the vehicle and headed out of town.

'Where to this time?' asked Dad wearily.

'Barabattia.'

'What is it like?'

'I don't know,' I said irritably. 'We'll just have to wait until we get there, and then make the most of it.'

Poor Dad closed his eyes in resignation. He had once weighed sixteen stones, but he had faded away before my eyes, and was now just skin and bones.

The New Year had started; it looked like being a far from happy one for all of us.

Chapter 6

⚜

Barabattia turned out to be a Gurkha village where several of the inhabitants were old soldiers who clung tenaciously to their allegiance to the British. In this they provided a sharp contrast to the Burmese, who for the most part refused to harbour us for fear of reprisals from the Japanese. I could not blame the Burmese for their attitude, though at the time it distressed me. The Japanese had come to Burma as liberators and though the British colonial yoke had never been particularly brutal, it was only natural that the Burmese should rejoice when it was lifted. By the time they discovered they had exchanged one set of conquerors for another it was too late. Besides, though they quickly learned to loathe their new masters, this did not particularly dispose them to love their former ones. To expect them to risk their lives so as to help people who they felt were better out of the country and who had never been welcome there in the first place, was to ask too much of human nature. All the same, it was hard not to compare them unfavourably with the Gurkhas, who never for a moment doubted where their duty lay. We were their friends, we were in need, and so they gave us shelter.

Having settled Dad in, I returned to Maymyo to collect the few items I had left behind. With Cocky perched on my shoulder, and the two dogs trotting faithfully beside me, I pushed my cycle, festooned with pots, pans and the contents of the larder, along the five miles of deeply rutted cart track that led to Barabattia. I was so worn out when I got back that I lay down on the ground, devoutly hoping it would be my last move for a very long time.

My new home was a large shed with a zinc roof, which had served as a school. Into it were herded eight hundred people, many of whom were total strangers. But there were also some familiar faces from the past with whom it was pleasant to compare experiences.

Conditions were primitive to say the least, but it was away from the bombers' target and for that we were grateful. Fortunately, Dad and I were allocated a space at the far end of the building, near a window looking out on to a veranda, which meant he had the benefit of fresh air and a slight breeze. We had all been shunted from pillar to post so often that we had learned that moaning got one nowhere; one had to pull together, grin and bear it. And so we coped as best we could, cooking over a pile of wood between two bricks, and making the place as clean as possible.

Inevitably, it was not long before my professional services were in demand, and once again I became a kind of unofficial district nurse. Maymyo was still being bombed, and although Barabattia was not directly affected, bomb casualties kept arriving. My time was fully occupied treating them in addition to those in the schoolroom who fell ill, not to mention the Gurkhas who were also coming to me with various ailments.

As food became scarcer, so the amount of sickness began to increase. Undernourished and with little resistance to disease, people regularly suffered from dysentery and malaria, while the slightest scratch turned into a gaping sore. They were the most common complaints, but no general practitioner could have had such a wide variety of illnesses to deal with. At the end of each day I was worn out, for although the village was relatively small it was densely populated, and to visit my patients scattered around it involved walking several miles.

It was a cause of constant regret to me that Dad would never place his medical knowledge at my disposal at a moment when it would have been of such tremendous help. I would describe the symptoms of an illness and ask him to give me a diagnosis, but he always refused. I tried to argue with him, and reminded him of the Hippocratic Oath by which he had sworn to devote his life to the healing of the sick, but he remained unmoved. Nothing I could say would make him budge or even discuss the issue. I did not know why he adopted this attitude, as it was totally alien to his nature. I suppose his own age and sufferings had finally broken his spirit; it seemed that he could kindle no spark of interest in what went on around him. He was so different to the man who had first started my own enthusiasm for medicine by taking me on his rounds when I was a small girl, describing the various illnesses and their treatment, and encouraging me to ask endless questions.

It was all the more heartbreaking, for when Dad developed diabetes and I could not obtain insulin, it was an old Gurkha woman who saved his life. She told me to soak some *bhindi* (a plant we know as kidney vetch or ladies' fingers) in water over night to extract the syrup, and to make him drink this. I did not know what medicinal qualities it had, but somehow it did the trick and controlled his sickness.

Then one morning I was visited by a man called Bahadur, who was the head of a well-to-do family. He was not the most popular person in the district, and I did not altogether trust him. He spoke fluent Japanese, and mingled a little too freely with them for my liking, although I had no evidence that he was sympathetic to their cause. Trying to be charitable, I hoped that, like me, he merely used them to his own advantage whenever the opportunity arose. Not that it mattered much one way or the other. I made it a rule that everyone should be treated equally, and no one refused my help, for the least sign of discrimination would have stirred up antagonisms in such a close-knit community. Besides, I feel strongly that the function of the doctor is to heal, not to pass judgement on a patient's actions or opinions. I will not pretend that I have always lived up to that precept myself, but I have tried to, and have only broken the rule under almost intolerable stress.

'My two sisters are very sick,' Bahadur announced. 'Please help them.'

I went to his home and immediately realised that they were suffering from typhoid. This was extremely worrying and not only for them, for in our overcrowded conditions the disease could spread like a fire in dry gorse.

They were not the easiest patients to nurse, and my problems were made more difficult by the fact that the house was so cluttered with furniture that there was hardly room to move. The sisters would persist in wearing saris containing yards and yards of material, of which they seemed to have an inexhaustible stock; there were always several hanging up to dry. All these were potential health hazards, and I made Bahadur get rid of most of them and move everybody out of the house but the two sisters. Despite strong family protests, I insisted on the sisters having separate cooking pots and cups, saucers and cutlery. In short, I put them in total quarantine.

I spent hours each day at their bedside. Bahadur tried to thrust money on me, but I refused. I had made it a rule that I would only take food and goods in return for my services, and I declined to make an exception in his case. In fact, it suited me well not to do so; because of his rather dubious relations with the Japanese, he always seemed able to get hold of items of food which were unobtainable elsewhere. Some of these he passed on, which enabled me to keep Dad reasonably well fed.

The sisters took a long time getting better, but they eventually made a complete recovery. Bahadur was effusive with his thanks and assured me that one day he would repay me properly. It proved not to be an empty promise. But for him I would not be here to relate my story.

Gradually I settled down into a well-organised routine. To show their appreciation, the people in the schoolroom, assisted by some of the Gurkhas, built me a small surgery of cow dung and pieces salvaged from ruined huts. I was so overcome that I insisted on having a formal opening ceremony at which I buried a religious medallion in the mud floor. I was now more than content to see the war out in Barabattia. The Japanese left us well alone, while the rumble of distant bombs was a constant reminder that it would not be overlong before the British arrived to relieve us.

And so the days passed into weeks, the weeks into months. Then without warning, my little world collapsed around me.

I received an urgent request to go into Maymyo to attend a woman who was a member of the Aga Khan's sect, and thus a strict Mohammedan who observed purdah. She was expecting her first child. I packed my kit and told Dad I would be away for at least three days. I delivered the baby on 7th September 1943, in the middle of an air raid. It was a date I can never forget. Having seen mother and child comfortably settled, I made plans to return to Barabattia, but first I had to call on a local doctor to get some ergot for my patient. As I was leaving his surgery a military car drew up alongside me and a member of the Kempetai, the Japanese equivalent to the Gestapo, leaped out. 'You are under arrest!' he shouted.

'What on earth for?' I asked in amazement, but he did not bother to answer; he simply bundled me roughly into the back of the car, where another policeman twisted my hands behind my back and snapped on a pair of heavy steel handcuffs before putting a blindfold over my eyes. Even in that moment of terror I could not help thinking how odd it was that the Japanese attached so much importance to their victims not knowing where they were being taken. I was clammy with apprehension. The scene was a little too close for comfort to the gangster films I had seen in Rangoon in the old days. Was I going to be shot and then tossed out of the moving car into a monsoon ditch, where I could lie for days without being found?

'What is this all about?' I said, trying hard to sound indignant, but a sharp blow across my face quickly silenced me. We drove the rest of the forty miles to Mandalay in absolute silence. Alone with my thoughts, I could not help wondering what information the police had received to make them take this dramatic action. I racked my brains to think of something, but could not recall anything likely to arouse their suspicions.

It was not a comfortable trip. I was perched uncomfortably

between the two policemen and as the car swerved I was thrown against them. They showed their displeasure at such physical contact by hitting me in the ribs.

I had never expected to be pleased to arrive in prison, but I felt only relief when the car came to a halt and I was hauled out, to hear the clanging of iron gates, before the car slowly moved forward again. Then the gates were shut. When the blindfold and handcuffs were removed I realised I was in Mandalay prison. I again asked why I had been arrested, but all I got in response was another blow. I was forcibly propelled into a small office where a Japanese officer was sitting stiffly behind a large desk.

'I demand to know why I have been brought here,' I said.

He looked at me and answered: 'You are a spy for the British.'

'That is rubbish! Ask any of the people in Barabattia and they will tell you I do nothing but nurse the sick.'

'You are lying,' he said, in a very matter-of-fact voice.

I pleaded with him to allow me to contact my father who was a sick man, and would be worried to death at my sudden absence. I added that there were also many other people who depended on my presence. They would die without my care.

The officer was totally unmoved, he simply gestured with his head and the two men who had arrested me grabbed my arms and pulled me out. I was tossed into a tiny, foul-smelling cell, with a small barred window overlooking a filthy courtyard. There were no facilities for washing and no toilet.

I was bewildered by this sudden turn of events. I knew I was not a spy, so why were the Japanese so adamant? I had been through it all before, and had finally convinced them that I was innocent. Would I be able to do so again? I felt sure I could. I sat with my knees clasped in my hands, my back resting against the dank wall, confident, given the opportunity to explain and to call witnesses, that I could convince them they had made a foolish mistake.

It was clear that the Japanese were in no great hurry to settle the matter. I was left in the cell the entire night and most of the next day without a soul coming near me. Then late the following evening the door was flung open, and two guards dragged me to my feet and marched me off for questioning.

Not that 'questioning' proved to be the right word. Certainly the officer sitting at the desk asked me none, instead he kept reiterating: 'You are a spy. We have proof. You must tell me everything.' I could only keep denying the allegation, parrot fashion. Listening to my own voice I knew it sounded unconvincing.

The session lasted no more than half an hour, then, with a brusque wave of his hand, the officer signalled to the guards to take me away. Next night the interrogation was much more severe. And so it went on. Apart from the times that I was taken out of my cell for questioning, I spent thirty-one days in solitary confinement.

It was not until much later that I learned what it was that had led to my arrest. My mother had written to me through the Red Cross, telling me that I had been awarded the George Medal for my work in Taunggyi. The Japanese censors had intercepted the letter, and assumed that this must be some kind of military decoration. Putting two and two together, the authorities jumped to the conclusion that I was a British spy who had been rewarded for undercover activities. The assumption was, perhaps, not wholly ridiculous. Given half a chance I could have pointed out the truth, but as the reason for their behaviour was never explained to me, I was not in a position to say anything that would allay their suspicions.

At that time of the year the temperature in Mandalay was often 104 degrees in the shade. My cell became as hot and steamy as an orchid grower's greenhouse, making sleep impossible. It also became the home of swarms of voracious mosquitoes which revelled in their helpless target. In no time at all I was completely covered in bites. They did not miss an inch of my skin. At night I used to take off what was left of my dress and use it as a pillow on the floor, so I had no protection whatsoever. I thought ruefully that I looked very much like one of the smallpox cases which I had manufactured to deceive the Japanese many months before. But there was nothing imaginary about my bites. They itched so much that I could not resist scratching them. This, as I knew perfectly well would be the case, only made them worse, for once the skin was broken they quickly festered and became open sores.

Every morning the small aperture in the door would be opened by a faceless guard who pushed through half a coconut shell containing a spoonful of rice and a piece of salted ginger. I also received half a shell of water which I could either drink or wash in. I was left alone for so long at a time that I sometimes feared I would go mad. To keep my mind occupied I sang hymns, said my prayers, and worked out problems in mental arithmetic. Often at night the rain came bucketing down, beating a monotonous tattoo on the roof and ground outside until I felt each drop was a blow on my head. I decided to use the noise as a cover to try to find out a little more about the rest of the prison, and so I began to call out loud enquiries about other prisoners; or in fact to sing out, for I actually sang my questions in order to mislead my captors. I used the music of any song that come to mind, and improvised the words so as to include requests for information. Clearly my captors thought the privations had affected my reason, as they made no attempt to silence me. Looking back it must have seemed like a scene from an opera, though more comic than grand: a solitary woman, covered in filth and bites, wearing a dress that was in tatters, standing at the window singing at the top of her voice: 'I am Helen Rodriguez. Are there any Europeans here?'

At least it worked. I learned that there were two other British prisoners in the adjoining cells, and in the musical exchanges they managed to tell me that a Catholic priest was also held in the jail.

Late one night, at a time when my resistance was at its lowest, the cell door was flung open. I was seized by the arms, dragged along the corridor, and pushed into a brilliantly lit room where I was confronted by an officer sitting behind a big, bare table. I was virtually naked, as the guards had not even given me time to slip on my dress. The two guards thrust me into a chair and stood menacingly behind me.

'You must tell me everything about the spy group,' said the officer.

'I cannot tell you anything, for the simple reason I have nothing to tell you,' I answered truthfully.

'You are number six in the ring,' he said with vast self-assurance.

I threw up my hands in a gesture of despair. 'I don't know what you are talking about. Believe me, I am telling the truth.'

The officer obviously did not believe me, for he motioned with his head and the two guards began beating me on the shoulders, the back of the head and neck with the flat of their bayonets. My skull felt as if it was bursting, but through the blaze of pain I could hear his voice repeating in a patient tone: 'You must tell me everything. The British left you behind on purpose so that you could spy. That is so?'

'It is not so. I volunteered to stay and look after my patients.'

Again a succession of blows rained down on my head and shoulders, and as the questions were repeated over and over again, I could only shake my head dumbly. I have no idea how long it went on, but it seemed an eternity before he signalled to the guards to take me back to my cell.

The same routine continued night after night with my interrogators becoming progressively more brutal. Lighted cigarettes were stubbed out on my bare arms and legs. Whenever my head slumped down, it was jerked upwards by the hair. I could only sit there and repeat until I was hoarse that they had made a dreadful mistake. I was not a spy. I was a nurse. My denials were taken as evidence of my stubbornness, and only brought the bayonets into action again. When they tired of these, they produced more refined methods of loosening my tongue. With a pair of pliers, they began to tear out my finger nails, one by one. All the time the officer was mentioning names which meant nothing to me. They were, he insisted, the names of the people I worked with. It was no use denying everything; they knew.

When I was returned to my cell, bruised and burning, I lay on the floor, thanking God that I did not know any spies. If I had I was not sure I would not have betrayed them. Then, at times, I found myself wishing I really had been a spy so that I would have had something to confess.

As the sessions continued, it became apparent the officer was losing his patience, while the guards now seemed to be beating me for the sheer fun of it. Then one night I was left alone. I thanked God my ordeal was over. It was not. In the morning the officer stormed into the cell and forced me to the small window overlooking the recreation yard.

'Look,' he shouted. 'You will now see what is going to happen to you if you do not tell the truth.'

To my horror, a group of people were led out and lined up against the wall opposite. A white bandage with a red spot in the centre was tied around their heads. Then they were shot dead in front of me.

I had never witnessed anything so cold-blooded or more demoralising. I was petrified with fear and tried to turn away, but my head was presed back towards the window. I was in despair; I had told the truth, and had just been beaten and tortured that much harder. What do I have to do to convince you, I thought.

Shaking uncontrollably, I turned to the officer and said: 'Why don't you shoot me? And when you have done that you had better shoot my father too, because there will be no one to look after him.' By then I had resigned myself to death; even worse, would positively have welcomed it.

Without uttering another word, the officer stormed out of the cell and the door clanged behind him.

The same ghastly spectacle was enacted two or three more times; I am not exactly sure on how many occasions I was forced to look out of the window as people were executed. Then the shootings and the torture stopped without any explanation being given. As the two halves of coconut were pushed through the grill, the guard said: 'You can go out later.'

I could not believe it. It must be some new and particularly cruel punishment for my recalcitrance. Apart from the trips to the torture chamber I had not been allowed to set foot outside the cell. Yet, when I had eaten my spoonful of rice, the door opened. I half crawled along the corridor into the yard. The first thing I saw was a well with a bucket and rope standing beside it on the brickwork. I could think of nothing but drenching my body with water to ease the agonising pain that seared through every joint and muscle, and I ran over, dropped the bucket into the well and poured the contents over my head.

A sentry snatched the bucket out of my hands, and an officer who was standing nearby said: 'If you want to bathe you must do it in front of the priest.'

'That I will never do,' I shrieked.

He shrugged his shoulders as if it was a matter of no great importance. 'He would not notice.'

My eyes followed his to where the priest was standing. He was a tall, emaciated man with long, auburn hair and a beard that made him look Christ-like, but he was totally out of his mind. His vestments were ripped to shreds, and he was swallowing the beads on his rosary. I tried to speak to him, but could not understand a word he said. He just stood there, looking for all the world like an El Greco portrait of a tortured monk. Later, when I was let out of my cell again, I asked one of the other prisoners about the demented priest. He told me that he was an Italian from the oilfields, who had been tortured so badly that his reason had deserted him. He now did and said everything possible to renounce his religion, but had too little grasp on reality to do even that with any consistency.

The break in my interrogation was very brief indeed, and I shall never understand why my gaolers allowed it. Soon the nightly questioning and torture began again. I lost all track of time. I became so feeble that my brain ceased to function, and I actually looked forward to facing the firing squad; a few seconds of terror, and it would all be over. I would be at peace. Then to my surprise, I was left alone to rot in my squalid cell. I lay on the floor with my eyes focussed on the door waiting for it to be flung open and for the guards to drag me out to the courtyard to be stood against the wall, where I had been forced to witness the death of so many others. But it remained closed for several days and nights.

Gazing at the door became an obsession; I was mesmerised by it. I wanted it to open, yet at the same time I feared it. When it finally did burst open one night, I steeled myself for the inevitable – a renewal of the torture – but when I was taken to the brightly lit room the officer simply said: 'You are to face trial before a tribunal.' He did not elaborate, but gestured for me to be led away. I was thrown back into the cell and left to reflect on what exactly his words meant. A sham trial, I presumed, followed by the formal sentence of death. At least the trial would be brief, and the outcome even quicker.

When the day of my trial arrived, I was escorted to a makeshift courtroom. There, to my astonishment, I saw Bahadur, the man whose sisters I had cured of typhoid. He whispered to me: 'I am your interpreter. Do not say a word. I will talk for you. I will explain how you have dedicated yourself to the sick. You saved my sisters. You are no spy. You must trust me.'

I nodded dumbly; in the circumstances there was nothing I could do but place my life in his hands. Not that I had much hope that his words could help. I had protested my innocence loudly and indignantly from the outset, and not been believed. What reason was there to suppose the members of the tribunal would be open to persuasion by Bahadur?

Not knowing a word of Japanese, I had no idea what he was saying in his long speech to the officers sitting on the dais above me. I had even less idea what effect they were having on his audience, for the expressions of the Japanese remained totally inscrutable. No one nodded, or made a note. They just sat impassively; perhaps not even listening.

My month-long ordeal ended as abruptly and as inexplicably as it had begun. The members of the tribunal retired, and when they returned I stood up, while the presiding officer jabbered something in Japanese. A touch on the shoulder from one of the guards standing behind me indicated that I was to leave the court. I was bemused; I had no idea whether I had been found guilty or not. Only the smile on Bahadur's face gave me reason for hope.

Without another word being uttered I was led out, dumped into the back of a lorry and driven to Maymyo, where the temperature was forty degrees below the bake-house heat of Mandalay. With only my torn and tattered dress to cover me, I shivered until my teeth rattled. I tried to talk to the guard, but either he could not speak Burmese or he had orders not to communicate with me, for he sat stiff and silent, as if I did not exist. The lorry stopped at the headquarters of the military police where my escort bundled me out, and led me to a room containing a small bunk where I was told to sleep. As I was so cold he kindly draped his coat around my shoulders.

Next morning I was given a towel, toothbrush and paste, and allowed to wash under an outdoor pump. After lining up with the soldiers for a meal I was led into an office where a sheet of paper and a pen was thrust in front of me. 'Sign that and you may go,' said the officer.

'What is it?'

'It's a statement saying that you have not been ill-treated or imprisoned. You will also give your word that you will not mention what has happened to anyone, not even your father.'

I shook my head. 'I refuse. If it were written in English so that I could read it, I might sign, but not otherwise. I might be swearing my life away for all I know!'

'It is not a trick. It simply says what I have told you.'

I had no idea why he wanted an assurance that I would not discuss my ordeal. So far as I could see it would not matter to the Japanese if I shouted the news from the roof tops. There was no one I could complain to officially, and if I talked about it to friends I would be wasting my breath; they all knew the kind of methods the Japanese adopted and how many people had suffered far worse than I had. He must have known this perfectly well himself, because he did not press the issue, and from his expression I even got the impression that he had a certain amount of respect for my defiance. Without any elaboration he said: 'You are free to go now.'

Chapter 7

I walked out into the street, and realised I had at least seven miles to walk before I reached Barabattia. The thought of seeing Dad again gave me a certain amount of strength, but I had only covered a few hundred yards before my legs gave way and I collapsed. I lay beside the road for about an hour until I felt strong enough to try again, but I only got a short distance before I fell again. After every fall the effort to rise and start again became harder, and at times I was actually crawling. By now it was getting towards evening, and I had still not encountered a single person to whom I could appeal for help. But I was too exhausted to wonder why so few people were about.

Finally I accepted that there was no hope of my reaching my destination that night. I curled up by the side of the road, intending to sleep until morning in the hope that the rest would give me strength to renew my journey. Then I heard the unmistakable clip-clop of horses' hooves. When I looked up I saw a shabby old cart approaching, with a lean, half-starved horse between the shafts. I shouted aloud to attract the attention of the driver who was perched on a small dickie seat. He reined in his horse and stopped beside me, surveying my bedraggled appearance. 'Get in,' he said.

I hesitated, and he asked, 'What's the matter?'

'I've no money on me.'

'It doesn't matter.'

I clambered into the back, slumped against the seat and closed my eyes.

As the horse plodded slowly in the direction of Barabattia,

With a group of nursing friends in Rangoon

Fishing in the Shan States

Japanese troops entering Taroy

A group of nuns of the Franciscan Missionaries of St May who
were interned during the occupation

my ears caught the deep-throated growl of an approaching aircraft. I understood then why the roads were so deserted: Maymyo was still under remorseless air attack.

As the sound of the plane grew louder, I knew it was a bomber coming in for an attack. Almost by instinct, I hurled myself out of the seat and landed in a deep ditch filled with slime and filth yelling as I did so for the driver to follow me. Seconds later there was a tremendous explosion and I was showered with mud and dust. When I scrambled out of the ditch, smelling like a pig sty, the cart was upside down with one wheel slowly spinning round. It had been shattered to matchwood, the horse was lying dead between the shafts, and the body of the driver had been hurled through the air and was lying in a crumpled heap twenty yards away.

It seemed most unlikely that the pilot had deliberately selected our humble cart as a target, and I could only assume that he had been intent on damaging the road. I suppose there was so little activity at that time, that anything moving might have attracted the bombers' attention. Not that the point was of any significance for the poor driver. There was nothing I could do for him. It seemed particularly unjust that he might not have died if it had not been for the time he lost as a result of his generosity towards me. I heard the engine recede into the distance, and waited in the shelter of some trees for it to return, but the sky remained mercifully silent. I set off again, walking in a deep trance. I was not even aware of my aching limbs or the pain from my injuries; I had become an automaton.

The bush telegraph that operated in the outlying districts was working with its customary efficiency even though I had seen nobody on the way, for the news of my release had filtered through to my friends in Barabattia and a small group, led by George Nicholas, was waiting to greet me at the bridge that crossed the stream on the outskirts of the village.

George looked at me, and said gently: 'Oh, poor Helen! Can you make it?'

'I've got this far, and nothing will stop me now,' I assured him, with a confidence I was not at all sure I could live up to. But with a couple of shoulders to lean on, I managed to hobble up the dusty road to the home of Joe and Mabel Daniels which was not far from the Gurkha settlement. It was a proper house with a roof and walls, and if that sounds a rather strange thing to rhapsodise about, I can honestly say that I had thought until a day or two before that the four walls of my cell would be the last that I would ever see. It takes a spell in an execution cell to awake one fully to the pleasures of life.

The Daniels were a delightful family; they fed me, bathed me, and put me to bed between clean sheets. Mabel told me that she had pleaded on my behalf with several Japanese officers to try to get me released, assuring them that I was not a spy, but they had shrugged their shoulders and said they were unable to help. It was something over which they had no control.

Joe and his two sons worked on the railway, and were given preferential treatment by the Japanese, who could not operate the vital system without their co-operation. It was Hobson's choice for the railway workers, for when the Japs arrived they had a complete list of all the drivers, shunters, firemen and guards. There was no question of their refusing to work; if they did so they knew that they would be shot and their families left to starve. On the other hand, if they worked they were paid quite generously and were allowed to rent empty houses. Special signs were put above their doors, guaranteeing them immunity from any form of harrassment.

Mabel, who had been a nurse with me in Rangoon many years before, had looked after Dad during my absence. She had done a wonderful job but I was shocked to see how far his condition had deteriorated. He was not only a very sick man, with diabetes and heart trouble, but he was desperately missing my mother. My own disappearance had done nothing to dispel his gloom. 'He seems to have lost the will to live,' Mabel said. 'Maybe he will pick up now he knows you are safe.'

Somehow or other Joe managed to borrow a cart, and drove

Dad and I to the village. There, to my great delight, I found the people had built me a small hut. It was not much to look at – a mud floor and bamboo roof – but it was somewhere of our own; it was a home. Even if it had been still more primitive, the fact that our friends had been at such pains to do this for us would have made me prize it enormously.

It took me several days to recover from my imprisonment and torture, and the very day I left my bed the Japanese swooped on the village and began rounding us up for the move to an internment camp. I had felt quite confident that I could recover my health in Barabattia, but I knew that I did not yet have the strength to cope with another move. My weight was down to little more than six stone, and I was jittery and depressed. Whilst I was away a trigger-happy soldier had shot Cocky, for no other reason than that it gave him a bit of fun. Another of my dogs had been put down, and the only pet remaining was Shaky, who trembled continuously from St Vitus's dance. In normal circumstances, I would have felt that these were no more than upsetting incidents, but in my state of mind they seemed intolerable burdens.

The Japanese were at their most uncommunicative and brutal; without a word of explanation they rounded us up like cattle, and gave the order to march. Some friendly Burmans were allowed to put Dad and his bed on to a bullock cart, the rest of us had to manage as best we could on our feet. I piled what I could into wicker baskets which I carried on my head, native fashion. And so I headed for my new home, wondering where it was and what it would be like. If any of us showed the slightest sign of lagging behind, the Japanese soldiers quickened our pace with none too gentle prods from their bayonets. We knew enough about their methods to be certain that if we broke down altogether and fell by the wayside, we would very quickly be spared further pain by a bullet or a killing thrust.

There had been little or no respite from the bombing while I was away, and this forced march of the refugees turned out to be a cynical attempt by the Japanese to increase their own safety.

They hoped our presence in the middle of a military strong point would be a deterrent to the bombers. It evidently did not occur to them that the pilots would have no way of knowing that we had been moved.

In peacetime, Maymyo had been a military cantonment, and since the occupation the enemy had taken over all the buildings and barracks evacuated by the British. The old Alexandra Barracks was their hospital, and they occupied the cavalry and artillery blocks. We were put into a wired-off compound containing several long, low buildings, one of which had been used by the signal unit of the Burma Army and was quite close to St Joseph's Convent, which I had attended as a small girl. The convent, which had once echoed with the sound of children's laughter, now housed members of the Indian National Army; prisoners of war who had been persuaded to switch their allegiance and fight alongside the Japanese. They believed that the independence of India would be the reward for their services. Their Commander-in-Chief was Subhas Chandra Bose, considered a traitor by the British and some Indians, a heroic freedom fighter by others. The railway yards were close by, and there was a big artillery unit based in All Saint's Church. We could hardly have been worse placed to avoid the attentions of the bombers. We were even deprived of our names, being given small pieces of wood with a number on it which served as an identity card. I was 41, the same number as the flat I now live in. Dad was 42.

I stood at the entrance to the long unlit building, and reflected that this was probably going to be my home until the British re-occupied Burma. It was a daunting thought, for God alone knew when that would be. Although we knew the Allies now apparently commanded the skies, we had no idea how the war on land was going. The building had clearly been used as a transit camp for soldiers and the accommodation was uncomfortably spartan; just low benches made of split bamboo all around the walls. The soldiers crowded us in and locked the doors. The benches would have to serve as beds and tables. We picked our spots, and settled down for our first night in captivity.

It was a night not entirely devoid of humour. I got up in the pitch dark to obey the call of nature, and when I returned I stumbled around trying to find my spot beside Dad. When I awoke in the morning I discovered to my embarrassment that I had snuggled up alongside a young married couple.

As time passed, we began to establish some kind of routine. It was obvious that, living as we were cheek by jowl with each other, strict discipline would have to be enforced if we were to survive. We appointed George Nicholas, who had worked in the land records office, as camp headman. I was detailed to supervise the medical side of things.

As Dad was so desperately ill, it was agreed that he should have a reserved space at the end of the room, so that he could look out of the window. I managed to get hold of some odd strips of cloth and canvas and erect a dividing curtain which gave him a little privacy.

The Japanese officer appointed commandant of the camp was a man for whom the word swine would be a flattering description. He had no interest in our welfare, seeing us simply as human sandbags to protect his men from air attack. He kept us on a starvation diet, and was deaf to my appeals for drugs and medicine. If anything, I think, he rather hoped we would die.

Our staple diet consisted of ground rice made into a thin pancake mixture, which was swilled around in a wok and then cooked over a wood fire. Those fortunate enough to have it added a pinch of bicarbonate of soda to make the mixture rise, and a little spice to give it some flavour.

I foraged around and managed to find a flat stone that was suitable for grinding rice. At first, it was an agonising process, as my nails had not yet grown after they had been pulled out in Mandalay and my fingers grew raw and bleeding through contact with the rough surface. In time they hardened, however, and I grew more expert at the work. The results were hardly savoury, but were much better than nothing; the un-appetising pancakes known as *doosai* were my staple diet for the first few weeks.

In these primitive conditions it was hardly surprising that the health of several of the prisoners began to decline alarm-ingly. There was little I could do about it, however. One of the more desperately ill was Mr J. A. King, who had four children, Doris, Marina, Richard and another girl I only knew as Snookey. It soon became apparent to me that unless he received prompt hospital treatment there was little or no chance of his living for long. He must have known the end was not far off, for one day he called me over to his cot. 'Helen,' he said, in a voice that was little more than a croak, 'will you promise me some-thing?'

'Of course,' I said. 'Anything I can do.'

'If I die, will you look after my children?'

I nodded dumbly. What else could I say to a dying man? It seemed an odd promise to have to give to a man whose Christian name I did not even know, but these were odd times. He died a few days later, and my promise had to be made good.

And so overnight I became Aunt Helen to four half-starved children. It was an enormous burden to shoulder, for Doris, the eldest, was an epileptic. The size of my family had increased, but the rations were cut, and we had to make the *doosai* go that much further. Dad was given the most appetising ones – not that these were anything very special – while the children and I made do with the rest. Thankfully, the children proved to be very resilient. My new-found family quickly overcame their sorrow at their loss and adapted to their new way of life.

Then, as if I did not have enough on my plate already, my family was enlarged some months later by the unexpected arrival of three more parentless children.

There was another internment camp close to Myitkina, filled with families who had been unable to fly out to India. Several of these were sent to Maymyo. Among them were Yvonne and Lesley Pugh, whose mother had died. Mrs Pugh had married a

Burmese named Pu, but had anglicised her name. There was also a third girl called Rosalind Anderson.

Rosalind was a beautiful, auburn-haired English girl of seventeen, who had suffered so much that it was hard to believe she was so young. Her feet were torn and bleeding and stripped of their flesh, while her head and legs were covered with maggot-infested sores. She was in a state of complete terror as a result of what she had been through. It was heartbreaking to see so young and pretty a girl reduced to such a pitiful condition.

Lesley and Yvonne, being half Burmese, were better able to adapt than Rosalind, who had enjoyed a life of comparative luxury until the occupation. Her father had been one of the best-known British figures in Burma, and owned the Minto Mansions Hotel in Rangoon. It was some time before Rosalind found enough confidence to tell me the full story of her adventures.

When the invasion came she, her mother and sister Paddy (Patricia), had gathered at Myitkina airfield in readiness to fly to India. Then the airstrip had been straffed and put out of action. Seven hundred people were left stranded. Rosalind and her family, as well as several others including an old lady of seventy-six and a mother with a baby and four small children, decided to walk to India.

A Kachin guide led them through the dense jungle along wild boar tracks for fourteen days until they reached Moguang, only to find the Japanese had already arrived there. During the trek they lit fires at night to keep off the wild animals. In a village near Monguang they found a half-ruined hut and lived there for three months during the monsoon, subsisting as best they could on rice and salt. They all suffered from malaria and skin ulcers. Mrs Anderson became very ill, and with no medicine or milk to keep her strength up, she did not survive for long. The old lady, the mother and baby, and Rosalind's sister Paddy one by one followed her. In all nine of the party died. For a girl of Rosalind's background to have survived such an ordeal was a tribute to her character and faith.

[133]

In the end, she told me, a treacherous Burman betrayed them to some Japanese soldiers who shot the one surviving male and then marched the girls off to the Japanese commander in Moguang. Fortunately, the Japanese major was a kindly man, who installed them in a house and made certain they were not molested by the Burmese or his own troops. They were not, however, excused work, and Rosalind and the other girls were made to cook and wait upon Japanese officers.

One night, she told me, a drunken Japanese officer chased her with a sword, and she described how she ran from hut to hut before finally shaking him off. When she reported the incident to the major, he had the man severely beaten.

Later she and several others were transferred to Maymyo to become members of my family. To return there and to find herself in such primitive conditions made her ordeal doubly painful, as much of her childhood had been spent at East Ridge, a magnificent country house with breathtaking views and gardens that were the pride of the neighbourhood. Before her family moved there it had been the boyhood home of the future Group Captain Peter Townsend, when his father was Commissioner of the Begu Division and a member of the Legislative Council.

About the same time, I took under my wing Mr 'Polly' Gibbs, whom I had known as a strapping, sporty type who worked in the Customs Department. Now he was too frail and ill to look after himself. Somebody had to accept responsibility for him, and there did not seem to be anybody else around who could do it. Including Dad and myself, I now had ten mouths to feed.

Those fortunate enough still to have any money were allowed to send out for food, but those who had none were left to cope as best they could on the muck our captors provided. My nursing experience was in such demand that I was able to supplement our diet with a few extras given in exchange for my services, while Mabel Daniels never failed to provide a little extra whenever she could spare it.

[134]

Then things took an unexpected turn for the better. I was allowed out occasionally to visit people in need of medical attention, being the only person permitted to leave the camp. I had to give detailed information to the camp commandant about where I had been, and what I had done. I knew that at first they checked to make sure I was telling the truth, but as time passed they accepted my honesty or lost interest, and stopped questioning me. Eventually I was allowed to go pretty much when and how I pleased. All I had to produce for the sentry was my small wooden identity tag. My new freedom of movement meant I was able to scrounge the odd bit of extra food, and, just as important, bits and pieces of furniture and household goods to improve my corner of the barracks.

Slowly, Rosalind's terrible sores began to heal, although I knew she bravely accepted that it would be a long time before the disfiguring holes completely disappeared. Strange as it may sound, the maggots, horrible though they were to look at, had played a part in restricting the infection. They kept the wounds clean and they acted as a primitive form of antiseptic. Rosalind was sent to work in the military hospital, dispensing drugs and tending the Japanese wounded. She took advantage of her function to steal small quantities of medicine.

Winter was fast approaching and there was an urgent need to obtain timber to close in the veranda. In the evenings I would wander around outside the camp, picking up the occasional bolt and nail, a pane of glass here, a sheet of tin there. I even began to look forward to the air raids on nearby Maymyo, for as soon as the sirens wailed I would be off through the gates, saying I had a patient to attend to. Instead of ministering to the sick, I would go looting and return with great loads balanced on my head like a coolie. The guards can hardly have failed to notice what I was doing, but I suppose they reckoned that, if the commandant allowed me to leave the camp, it was no business of theirs what I brought back with me.

In this manner I collected window frames, more glass, planks

[135]

of wood, and all sorts of things that could be put to use improving our conditions. I spurned nothing: lengths of rope, a broken blind, an old sack. All were gold dust. I found some sheets of zinc, and hammered at them until I had manufactured a small but efficient waist-high stove. In time, I was able completely to enclose our portion of the hut. As the raids happened regularly day and night I had plenty of opportunities to acquire useful material, and soon we had a table to eat off, and jars in which to grow mint, chillies and spices. I even managed to get a spoon and fork for Dad.

Although the camp was never directly hit by bombs, the building would shake from roof to floor from the explosions. My small compartment had to be rebuilt more times than I care to remember, and frequently my prized pots of spices were shattered. Luckily it was no great task to repot them. Rosalind presented me with a small plaster statue of the Virgin Mary which I kept near my bed, and which she swore gave us strength and courage to survive. During all the raids, it never once fell over.

Not all the internees were in our building; some were housed in old barrack blocks and adjoining huts. Soon communities sprung up within the main community. There were Catholics, Protestants, Jews and Armenians, and throughout the day there usually seemed to be a service being conducted by one or other of the groups. In this way, they were able to preserve their identity and customs, and keep their spirits up.

Considering so many of us were herded together in a confined area, there was surprisingly little bickering. There was always a selfish minority who would try to better their lot at the expense of others, but we had our own rough and ready methods of justice when they were caught out. It was harsh, immediate, and very effective, for it did not take long for even the most selfish to realise that if they did not work for the common good they would only be punishing themselves. They found the stuffy, overcrowded quarters were the loneliest place on earth if they were cold-shouldered and sent to Coventry.

The camp commandant got no more lenient as time wore on – indeed, if possible, he became more cruel and unfeeling. I learned from other prisoners that he was in the habit of ordering six young girls to be sent up to the officers' mess. So far our block had escaped his attention, but I knew it would only be a matter of time before his interest focussed on it. Sure enough, a soldier arrived one evening and asked me to make six young girls available.

'You can go back and tell the commandant he is wasting his time,' I said.

The soldier ignored me and held up two hands, one showing five fingers, the other one. 'Six girls,' he insisted.

I told him to wait while I went to George Nicholas, who called a meeting of all the mothers affected. Without exception, they were adamant; no young girl from our block would go to the officers' mess.

I considered myself one of the mothers because I now had a family of my own to look after. I knew only too well how much weight to attach to the messengers' assurances that the girls would be required to do no more than wait at table. I had learned from luckless victims who had already been to the mess just what the duties of a waitress entailed.

I returned to the waiting messenger and said firmly: 'You can go back and tell the commandant that he is not getting any of our children. If he must have women, he can take us in their place.' I hoped that he would decline the offer, as none of us looked particularly suitable for the sort of entertainment he had in mind. Whether we would get away with our defiance I did not know – I was much more alarmed than I appeared to be – but these children were my responsibility and so long as I lived I would not let them be made the playthings of drunken and lecherous Japanese officers.

The commandant may not have been best pleased but he was obviously a man who considered any women was better than none. Rather to our surprise, he accepted the compromise.

We called for volunteers and selected half a dozen of the more stalwart women for the disagreeable and possibly dangerous outing. I insisted that I should be one of the participants – after all, it was largely my obstinacy which had got us into this mess in the first place. And so we set off. We were hardly a bevy of beauties capable of arousing passion in even the most licentious of soldiery; our clothes were torn and patched, and we were all undernourished. We trudged up the hill to the attractive bungalow which used to be the home of the Reverend Mr Slater, but now served as the officers' mess. Despite the military occupation, the rose garden of which Mr Slater had been so proud still thrived in all its glory.

Faces remain, but names fade with the passage of time. The only name I can recall among the volunteers was Mary Tun Hla Aung, an extremely attractive American woman, married to a policeman who was jailed elsewhere.

It was sheer torture serving steaks and fried fish to the officers sitting around the long table. Strange as it may seem, one of our favourite pastimes in the hut was to talk about the meals we would have when the war was over. We would fantasise for hours over the dinner parties we would give, and the menus we would present to our guests. It was a kind of torture, and yet we enjoyed it. I for one could often taste the make-believe meals I conjured up in my imagination. When we actually saw the real food on the table, our mouths watered; but our excitement passed unnoticed by the officers, who washed down their meal with measure after measure of hot *sake*, the 'sacred' wine of the Japanese, which they drank from dainty porcelain cups. The more they drank the noisier they became, and when the last plate was cleared away the commandant staggered drunkenly to his feet and indicated that we were to join them in the living room. It was typical of the strange standards observed by the Japanese that we were excused washing up; such a task was far too menial for women who were deemed worthy to provide comfort to fighting warriors.

By now the officers were all very drunk and boisterous. One began to make strenuous advances towards Mary, while another focussed his glazed eyes on me. A third seemed to be having a little trouble making his mind up. Their behaviour was terrifying. Until then I had thought the Japanese were too conscious of the importance of face to make a spectacle of themselves. Now they were like animals, staggering around and shouting their heads off. What made it worse was the fact that none of us could understand a word of their crazy ranting; we had no idea what debauch they might be planning.

I had already made up my mind that, no matter what happened to me afterwards, no Jap was going to rape me – for rape it would have had to be, I had no appetite for seduction scenes. As I looked round in anxiety, I noticed that Mary Tun Hla Aung had a brooch with a small stone in it, which was fastened to her dress by a long, sharp pin. I edged towards her, and whispered: 'Give your brooch to me. Then get everybody to move over to the window and, when I give the word, jump out and run like hell.'

Nothing happened immediately, except a lot of drunken pawing. It was obvious that they needed more *sake* to bolster their courage before they took the final step. Soon they went out to get more drinks, leaving behind the officer who had set his cap at me. He moved towards me, and I sensed that the moment of crisis was near.

With a drunken lurch, he grabbed hold of me. 'Now!' I shouted at the top of my voice, at the same time sticking the pin of the brooch through his tunic into his chest. It must have sunk in an inch or more. He let out a scream that turned into a bellow of rage as we hurled ourselves out of the window.

Mr Slater's roses may have been his pride and joy, but I cursed them in no uncertain manner as I landed in the middle of one particularly thorny bush. As I picked myself up I saw the officer, his long curved samurai sword unsheathed, struggling to clamber out of the window. 'Run for your lives,' I shouted, and I meant it; his sword was flashing in the moonlight, lopping off imaginary heads as he struggled to his feet and began to race after us.

The others went off like hares chased by whippets, but I was at a disadvantage; my leg wound had never healed properly and I had a pronounced limp. The sight of that long-bladed sword, however, capable of slicing my head off at one stroke, gave wings to my heels. I ignored the pain and kept going. He was gaining on me, though. My heart was pumping furiously, and my lungs felt as if they would burst. I saw the others had escaped through the gate of our compound and were hiding behind a large, brick-built kiln by which the sentries used to keep themselves warm at night. Behind me I could hear the sound of my pursuer's boots pounding the ground, and his enraged voice bellowing, 'Stop! stop! stop!'

I shot past the astonished sentry, hurled myself on to the ground behind the stove, and waited, heart in mouth, to see what would happen next. To my immense relief, the sentry closed the gate and stood there with his bayonet pointing menacingly at my pursuer. The drunken officer halted in his tracks, looked at the bayonet and demanded to be let through, but the sentry vigorously shook his head. For once I was grateful for the iron discipline of the Japanese army. The sentry had orders not to allow anyone to enter the camp without permission, and that applied as much to his own officers as to anyone else. He may, of course, also have felt some sympathy for the fleeing women and disapproved of their drunken pursuer. In any case, although the sword-wielding drunk continued to shout and swish the air with his sword, the soldier remained unruffled and refused to budge. Eventually the officer sheathed his sword and weaved his way unsteadily back to the mess, muttering and cursing to himself as he did so.

Naturally the men were waiting up for us, unable to sleep through worry. George Nicholas asked: 'What was all the rumpus about, Helen? What has happened to you all?'

'We'll tell you in the morning,' I replied wearily. It was nearly two o'clock, and we were totally exhausted. Even though we felt some slight pride at our achievement, we were in no mood to recount at that late hour the ordeal we had been through, not to mention the even greater one we had narrowly avoided, thanks to Mary's brooch.

In the morning I told the whole story to George and expressed my fear that the entire camp might be subjected to reprisals because I had treated an officer like a pin cushion. The Japanese were unpredictable but if they felt their pride had been offended their vengeance might have been fearful. George was so incensed that he called for an immediate meeting at which it was decided that the best line of defence was attack. To forestall any attempt at revenge, they submitted a written complaint to the commandant. In strong and formal language, they protested that the women must not be regarded as chattels, and reminded the commandant that his conduct, and that of his fellow officers, was contrary to the Geneva Convention; they also threatened to draw it to the attention of the International Red Cross.

That done, we settled down to wait apprehensively for an explosive Japanese reaction. It never came. Whether the threats had some effect, or whether the Japanese officers felt some shame over their behaviour, I will never know. The important thing was that there were no more requests for 'waitresses', and there were no reprisals. Nevertheless, the commandant made his displeasure known, even though he did not make an appearance in the camp. He ruthlessly tightened the screws and food became even scarcer.

There was nothing more dispiriting for us – close to starvation as we were – than to see the living standards of the Japanese improving. Huge cattle trucks regularly arrived packed with bellowing cows, who could sense they were heading for the abattoir. The Japanese ate the meat and generously left us the bones. When the almost meatless morsels were handed over to us, Mr Nicholas, a most warm-hearted and generous man, forced himself to deprive others in order that the most needy could eat. He ruled that only those above sixty and below sixteen were entitled to the pickings from the bones, the rest had to be content with what was left. I boiled my ration of bare bones over and over again to make soup. Although it was not very filling, it was not without nutrition, certainly a great deal better than nothing.

Then the detested commandant was replaced by Captain Murano, a completely different man in every respect. He was a lawyer by profession, and although he now wore a uniform he still respected the traditions of his peacetime job. He was strict yet scrupulously fair; and above all he was approachable. His predecessor had kept himself entirely aloof from the prisoners. When I pleaded with the new commandant for drugs and medicine, or for permission for someone to see a doctor, he did his best to meet my requests.

With the Allied armies slowly but gradually coming nearer, there was little he could do to improve our rations. What food there was he needed for his own soldiers. He did, however, relax some of the more rigid orders that had existed for so long. Prisoners were allowed to leave the camp from morning until evening, which meant that they could find work and earn enough money to buy a little food, or barter precious belongings for salt, sugar or fruit. Occasionally, Kodama San would give me something from his own rations, but he had to be extremely careful as it would have been a court-martial offence if he had been caught.

During my rounds of the compound one morning, I noticed that the Japanese would not touch the lower half of a cow's leg, which included the hoof. These scraps were not passed on to Mr Nicholas, but instead tossed into a pile outside the slaughter house. When no one was looking I began to help myself to the occasional one. Nobody seemed to object, so I made it a regular habit. I carried the legs back to my quarters, where little Richard King would shave off the hairs with a piece of broken glass; his hands would be covered with cuts and blisters, but he never complained. I would then put the leg into the fire until I was able to knock off the hoof, after which I would chop it up into sections with an axe, and stew it for hours on end. It provided excellent jelly.

A Japanese tank in front of the pagoda

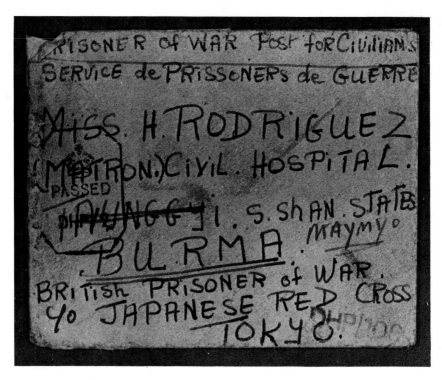

The envelope of my mother's letter which incredibly reached me
in Maymyo

My arm band from the prison camp

One problem was that the cooking took so long that there was usually an air raid before the stock was ready. It was a camp rule that all fires had to be extinguished immediately the sirens sounded as they would have provided ideal marker beacons on which the bombers could home in. Then, when the all-clear was sounded, the fires had to be rekindled, no easy task when the wood was sodden wet. But in the end the jelly was finished. It was those cows' legs which kept my family alive, week in, week out. They had no serious illnesses throughout the entire period of their internment.

Dousing the fires had another unfortunate consequence. While prison conditions brought out the best in most of us, it had the reverse effect on a small minority. They became human scavengers, and used the raids as a welcome opportunity to steal from their neighbours. Many times I returned to complete my cooking, only to find the contents of the pot were missing. Once I managed to steal a whole cow's tongue from the Japanese, a rare delicacy, but it vanished during an air raid. I did not feel that I was in a very strong position to complain; partly because I had stolen the tongue myself in the first place, but also as I was largely responsible for the 'fires out' order. It was I who had warned Mr Nicholas that they were drawing attention to our presence and should be extinguished in case of an attack. There had been grumbling at the time and I think some people would have felt that if I suffered because of the rule I had only been hoist with my own petard.

Another camp order was that we should all go to the deep slit trenches during air raids. These were waist-deep in water, and as raids often lasted three or more hours, people were falling sick through seeking shelter in places which should have afforded protection. Dad could not get as far as the trench in any case, and so I decided to take a stand and refuse to obey the order. Instead I spent the time under the table with my father.

Captain Murano was most put out. 'You must obey my orders like the rest, Miss Rodriguez. You *must* go to the trenches.'

'No. You go and stand up to your waist in water if you want to! I certainly am not going to. If you can't put a roof over the top I prefer to go under the table.'

Captain Murano again proved that he was a tolerant and reasonable man. I was allowed to get away with my defiance and, still better, bamboo covers were put over the trenches.

Dad, alas, was going downhill fast. He weighed less than half his normal weight, and it was only the thought of being reunited with Mother that kept him going. He was by nature a remote, scholarly man, who did not mix readily, preferring his own company to that of others. He loved reading, and sadly missed his well-stocked library at Craigmore. Hour after hour he would sit on his bed gazing vacantly into space. In the end I decided that, if he was to retain his sanity, it was essential to find him something to read. And so during my visits to Maymyo I collected any scrap of paper with printing on it, a page from a newspaper, an official notice, cartons, lists of instructions. . . . Even a laundry list would be better than nothing. I would give them to him and watch him sit transfixed as he read the same words over and over again. As my movements became less restricted, I scoured deserted homes in search of reading matter, and in time built up a small library. I seldom found complete books, often there was only a cover and a few pages, but it did not matter, Dad was delighted. It was pathetic to see how a man who had once prided himself on the amount he read, could be so easily satisfied. But prison does that to you.

As the months dragged wearily by and the hope of freedom seemed to grow more rather than less remote, discipline in the camp began to deteriorate. When people have high hopes, morale is high too; but when depression sets in they tend to adopt an 'Oh, what's the use' attitude. That happened at Maymyo. Captain Murano noticed it and sent for me. He said that as I was the only qualified nurse in the camp he was going to appoint me to be in sole charge of all hygiene. It would be up to me to ensure that all the camp regulations were strictly observed. I had to admit that the task needed doing, for it did not call for any very expert observation to see that people had become slap-dash in their personal habits.

I realised what a tough job I had been given. Because of my age a lot of the older people would take exception to my giving them orders. Somehow, however, they had to be jolted out of their apathy. My only hope of success was to be a martinet and a bully. People who had once been so meticulous in keeping themselves and their quarters scrupulously clean, had now become lazy and slovenly. The younger children were neglected, and the sick roll was beginning to rise. Swearing, in fact any bad language, had been taboo at Craigmore, it was something Dad just would not tolerate. Now I went to him and told him bluntly that I would have to break the golden rule and start swearing like a trooper. He was too sick and tired to care; he just nodded and said: 'You must do as you think fit, Helen, but don't let me hear you.'

Overnight I became a harridan: harsh, strict, and abusive to anyone who had the temerity to disobey me. I armed myself with a stout bamboo pole, and I wasn't slow to use it on anyone who slipped into dirty habits.

When I found anyone had used the drains as a toilet I handed out immediate punishment; when there was an outbreak of dysentery I ordered all the men who were fit to dig deep pits on the outside of the camp, and asked Captain Murano to see that piles of quick lime were regularly delivered. In this way, I prevented it spreading, and stopped any other illnesses which would have been encouraged by lowering the standards of hygiene. In addition, I made the men prepare rubbish pits in which all contaminated linen and refuse was to be buried. If any lice were detected I shaved heads bald. Some of the women, who considered their locks to be their crowning glory, protested volubly, but no exceptions were allowed. Some protested that they could pick the nits out themselves, but I knew better; in that heat and with everyone living on top of each other, the vermin would multiply overnight. I was also severe with people

[145]

who did not keep their beds clean, for once bugs got established it was the devil's own job to get rid of them.

I worked from early morning until late at night, and but for the children I think I would have gone mad. They helped me retain my sense of proportion and of humour. I played games with them, sang with them, and shared my prayers with them. I grew to love them as if they had been my own, and I think they loved me too. That at least I had to be thankful to the Japanese for. I was grief-stricken when the child who had suffered from epilepsy died, but nothing I did could have saved her. In addition to the fits, she was a victim of beri-beri. She needed hospital care. As for the other members of my brood, they had their ups and downs, but never anything serious. They suffered from toothache, lost the odd molar, had tummy upsets, and the occasional fever, but all in all they remained astonishingly fit and cheerful.

Richard King was an absolute godsend. He liked nothing better than to accompany me on my rounds, helping with dressings and plying me with endless questions. Although I was always Aunt Helen to them all, I knew that I had also to be a replacement mother and I did my utmost to bring them up with a proper sense of values. I impressed on them the unimportance of material possessions, and the importance of a firm religious faith, and I tried to instil in them the values of truth, honesty and loyalty; qualities which, if adhered to, would enable them to overcome all adversity. But I avoided being a Bible thumper. I stressed that they did not need to be religious in the sense that they always had to be going to church. God was everywhere, and I explained that I could just as well say my prayers at the foot of a pagoda as in a cathedral. Although young, in many ways much younger than their years indeed because they had missed so much formal schooling, they appreciated the fact that I was not lecturing or hectoring them. Without being pompous, I tried to set myself up as an example. They knew Dad and I had lost everything, yet they never heard us talk about it or lament the injustice of it all. I was not being high-minded or priggish, just practical. I knew the important thing was to survive, and to emerge a little the better for it. You could not do that by spending your waking hours thinking of what might have been and moaning about the unfairness of life.

I had become accustomed to the Japanese making decisions that were incomprehensible, and Captain Murano, for all his sophistication and decency, was no exception. Nothing surprised me more, however, than his decree that in future only Japanese and Burmese would be spoken in the camp. I suspect that the order came from on high, it was so unlike his usual attitude towards us. To make sure it was enforced, he sent a military interpreter into the compound to teach the children their new language. The arrival of the teacher relieved me of a host of problems; for the first time in months I found I had time on my hands because the children became devoted to him.

He in turn idolised them, although for the life of me I could not understand why, as they subjected him to every possible childish prank. He turned up every day as punctual as a Swiss watch to give his lessons, then he would take them for what he called a nature walk in the beautiful countryside around Maymyo. He was an incredibly sweet and knowledgeable man, who taught them a lot about the land; he knew every flower and tree, and the call of every bird. When the children returned they were laden down with bananas, peanuts, and sweetmeats, which he had bought from wayside sellers. He was only an ordinary soldier, and his purchases must have taken most of his pay, but the smiles on the faces of my family were more than enough reward for him.

Far from showing their gratitude in their behaviour, however, my mischievous brood let down his cycle tyres, loosened his saddle so that he fell off, hid his tools, and got up to all kinds of tricks that would have tested the patience of a saint. When he asked who had done so and so, or requested the return of his spanners or puncture outfit, they just looked at him, their faces beaming with childish innocence. Patiently he would smile and resign himself to a repeat performance during the next outing.

[147]

Children can be so cruel without realising it, and I let them know I did not find their antics at all funny by giving them a good whack with my bamboo pole. He genuinely seemed not to resent their behaviour, however; from the anguished look on his face when I hit them you would have thought the stick was being used on him.

With the uncanny receptiveness of children, they quickly picked up Japanese, and I was soon learning it from them. I had always had an aptitude for languages, and in a short time I was reasonably fluent. For want of anybody better qualified I was even appointed camp interpreter. I wished I had learned the language much earlier, for I discovered that our captors were much more receptive to requests if made in their own tongue. Somehow it did not seem to them so arrogant.

The strict discipline which I was imposing began to pay dividends, and slowly but perceptibly the compound became a harmonious and healthy community. Roads between the huts were swept clean, and everyone was on neighbourly terms. In the evening the women cleaned themselves and their children for social gatherings and prayer meetings, or just simple get-togethers. The men had stag meetings at which they yarned about old times and made plans for the future. The selfishness, which had once been such a trial, almost disappeared as people went out of their way to help each other. There was still the odd exception, but you will find a bad penny even in Utopia. Fortunately, the women were no longer pestered by the Japanese, as Korean prostitutes were now brought in to satisfy their physical needs. I felt sorry for the Korean girls, but grateful for their presence.

With more spare time on my hands, I began to reflect on the interrogation to which I had been subjected in Mandalay. I recalled that the Japanese officer had revealed the existence of a spy ring, and during the long questioning sessions had disclosed the names of people with whom I was supposed to have worked. They were names which had stuck in my memory. I found myself wondering whether I could contact them and help the Allied cause, as I frequently obtained valuable information about troop movements when I visited Maymyo.

I did not have to act as a spy to get my facts, on the contrary they were readily given to me. Maymyo, being 3000 feet above sea level, was used as a centre where battle-weary soldiers returning from the front could recuperate, and there was a tremendous amount of rail movement, especially at night. The Japanese relied on the railways, the efficient running of which was dependent on the large force of Anglo-Indians and Anglo-Burmans, who were allowed to continue in their peacetime occupations. Many of them, like the Daniels, were old friends, and during my visits they frequently passed on valuable information about troop build-ups, advances, retreats, and so on.

Try as I might, I was unable to get in touch with any of the people whose names I had kept locked in my memory for so long. I suppose it was naïve of me to imagine that I would be able to do so; if the Japanese could not find them with all their resources, what chance was there that I would succeed? I resigned myself to the fact that the information I got would never be used to advantage. My chance came, however, just when I had abandoned hope, and from a most unexpected source. One evening Bahadur, the interpreter from Barabattia who had saved me from the firing squad, arrived at the camp asking permission to speak to me on a very urgent matter. I was taken to the gate where a sentry stood close by, listening intently to what he had to say.

'My wife is in heavy labour and needs immediate assistance.'

'I will come straight away,' I promised.

The sentry, bored to hear it was nothing more important than another confinement, walked away and let Bahadur get on with the real purpose of his visit.

'There is a British officer nearby,' he whispered. 'He is very sick and hiding near the reservoir. He has no food and cannot contact anyone.'

'I will pack my bag and meet you here in a few minutes,' I

replied, remembering with some shame how I had once thought Bahadur was in the pay of the Japanese. He lowered his voice even more and asked me to meet him in a spot in the jungle not far from the camp. 'Bring food and medicine,' he murmured.

I collected my bag and met him at the pre-arranged rendezvous where he whispered: 'We must not walk together. I will go ahead and leave a trail. He is about seven miles from here.'

Following his trail in the semi-darkness was not easy, but eventually I caught up with him. He was waiting in a small clearing, and when I arrived he put a finger to his lips and imitated the call of a bird. We waited for several minutes before an emaciated figure emerged from the surrounding darkness. We shook hands, and the stranger introduced himself as Captain Ward. He said that he had been dropped by parachute with a transmitter some weeks previously with instructions to establish contact with the local resistance and report on Japanese troop movements. The whole operation struck me as being a little amateurish, as he seemed to have very little idea how to set about his task.

He was ravenously hungry, and when I handed him the hard-baked chapattis I had brought with me, he wolfed them down as if they were prime beef. He told me he was suffering from malaria. At times the bouts were so severe that he became unconscious, and often could not remember what messages he had sent out on his transmitter.

He was shivering badly and I gave him the medicine I had brought – M and B693, some creosote tablets for his dysentery and some bandages and lint. 'I will bring a blanket next time,' I promised.

We sat in the gloom talking quietly, and the mere fact that he was speaking English and establishing contact with someone who was willing to help, cheered him up a great deal. I told him I was prepared to pass on to him any information I received, and would try to make regular visits with food and medicine. Bahadur had also brought some hard-boiled eggs, so when the time came for us to leave the captain was in a much happier frame of mind.

On the way down a nervous Bahadur asked: 'What will you say to the sentry?'

'Don't worry. Just leave the talking to me.'

When the sentry stopped me, he said: 'How is the woman?'

'Mother and baby are doing fine,' I replied. 'A lovely boy. Seven pounds in weight.'

Behind me Bahadur beamed stupidly, looking for all the world like a proud father.

Once a week I visited the solitary soldier hidden away in his fox hole with his transmitter, and passed on what information I had picked up on my rounds. I had no difficulty in convincing the sentries that I was off on another errand of mercy. Confinements became a regular excuse, but the guards never expressed surprise at the sudden bulge in the birth rate. Perhaps they thought that I was in fact off to keep a romantic tryst and laughed to themselves at my thinking they were so credulous. If so, I know who had the last laugh.

Chapter 8

I kept up the clandestine visits for two months or more; always taking with me some chapattis, as hard as a rock but edible, and whenever possible some strips of meat which I fried, then boiled in salt water until they were like bits of leather. In the heat this was the only means of preserving meat, and I told Captain Ward to soak it for as long as possible before trying to eat it. Less frequently I managed to take him some hard-boiled eggs and the odd piece of chicken. But this was not the kind of diet on which he could survive indefinitely, and although I kept the malaria in check for some considerable time, his condition took a turn for the worse. He was a strange man in some respects; incredibly brave, always friendly, but never completely confiding. I suspect he did not entirely trust me. He eagerly accepted the information I passed on, but all he would say in return was that the British were doing well, and the end wasn't too far off.

Soon after my first meeting with Captain Ward I had the dubious privilege of being introduced to Chandra Bose, leader of the rebel Indian National Army. I say dubious, because in my eyes he was a traitor, although I think even then I realised that he must have appeared quite different to some of the Indian nationalists. Not many Indians supported him, however. Surprisingly few captured Indian soldiers joined his army, and some of those who did were at heart loyal to the British, simply seeing their new employment as an improvement on a life in a prisoner of war camp. Many had witnessed the harsh and degrading treatment meted out to those who remained loyal, and had no wish to share it. They had seen officers and sometimes other ranks locked away for months in cages that were scarcely big enough to house a dog. One can hardly blame them for wishing to escape such a fate, at the price of exchanging one foreign master for another.

The meeting with Bose came about in a rather odd manner. There was an English woman in the camp whose husband was an Indian doctor working in one of the Japanese hospitals. She was suffering from neurasthenia, and I pleaded with Captain Murano to allow her to live with her husband. Otherwise I said that I could not guarantee her sanity.

My request was obviously passed on to Chandra Bose, who must have suspected I was up to no good. The following day I was marched out of the camp by two soldiers and taken to a mansion which had once been the residence of a high-ranking official. There I was led into a room and confronted by an Indian.

'Do you know who I am?' he asked.

'I have no idea,' I replied in all honesty.

'Would you like to know?'

'It is a matter of complete indifference to me who you are.'

'I am Subhas Chandra Bose. Now do you know who I am?'

'No, I don't. We get very little news in the camp.'

He looked slightly put out by this not-entirely-honest reply but did not pursue the matter. Instead he asked me if it was true that I had advised the camp commandant to let an English woman leave the camp to live with her husband.

'Yes,' I replied. 'I did it because I think she will become deranged otherwise.'

'Will you give me a certificate to that effect?'

I immediately became suspicious that a trap was being set for me; he clearly thought I wanted to plant her in the hospital as some kind of informant and wanted documentary evidence of my guilt.

'I am a nurse, not a doctor, therefore I am not qualified to give a medical certificate,' I said.

Bose smiled, and asked me if I would like anything to eat or drink. When I refused, he said: 'I don't suppose you get oranges or sugar in the camp; would you like some?'

'I have learned to live without luxuries,' I said, though every nerve in my body screamed out to me to accept the offer.

When it became obvious he was not going to recruit me with bribes or blandishments, he signalled to the two soldiers to return me to the camp.

Bose was a strange man who aroused hatred or devotion, depending on where your allegiance lay. I saw him fleetingly from time to time, but never again to speak to. The meeting with him taught me one thing, however: I could never afford to lower my guard. There was always someone ready to report the slightest suspicious act and plenty of people eager to put the worst interpretation on perfectly innocent behaviour.

Some time later I made what was to be almost my last visit to Captain Ward, who was now a very ill man.

'I can't operate the set any longer,' he said. 'If I teach you how to use it, will you take it away with you?'

I was silent for a long time. 'Do you realise what you are asking me to do? I have a sick father, and a lot of children to look after. If I am caught I will be shot, and their lives endangered.'

As an additional obstacle, I pointed out to him that I was still on parole. I would be abusing the trust the Japanese had put in me. Of course I knew this argument had no real force – I was already abusing their trust and it was a bit late to start having a tender conscience at this point in the proceedings. Captain Ward kept on stressing how important the work was. It was Bahadur who finally convinced me it was my duty to take it. 'For the sake of all of us. We will stand by you. Do not worry.'

And so, with marked reluctance, I allowed Captain Ward to teach me how to work the battery set. When I was suitably efficient I arranged to collect the transmitter and take it back to camp.

I knew I had to be very wary, and not make the slightest mistake that would arouse the suspicions of the sentries and cause them to search me, so I killed a chicken – a great sacrifice

– drained some blood into a bottle, then packed my midwifery bag and presented myself at the gate. I told the guard I had been called out on an emergency confinement; he could not have cared less, and simply waved me through.

Bahadur was waiting at the usual spot, and once again accompanied me to the secret hideaway. I packed the transmitter into my box, covered it with bandages and pieces of cloth, and said farewell to Captain Ward. I felt extremely guilty leaving him, sick as he was, but there was no way I could help him. He told me not to worry, as he had been able to make contact with friends who would shelter him until he recovered.

I made my way back to the camp, my heart pounding so loudly I feared the sentry would hear it. The front of my dress was stained with chicken blood, on a scale which even the most unobservant person could not fail to notice, but the sentry looked at it with complete indifference.

'It was a very difficult delivery,' I said wearily, but I might as well have saved my breath. He was not remotely interested. I wished I had not gone to such great lengths to deceive him; getting blood stains out of a dress is one of the hardest tasks, especially when water is rationed.

In the seclusion of my cubicle I sat down and heaved a sigh of relief; I had got the set back safely, now all I had to do was find somewhere safe to hide it. Although it was a small portable set, there was no hiding place in my cubicle which would not be exposed by the most cursory inspection. Then I hit upon the idea of using Henny Penny.

I had managed over the months to collect four hens which provided me with much-needed eggs. Three were regular layers; Henny Penny on the other hand was a total loss. She did nothing but cluck noisily as she sat on an imaginary egg, but I lived in hope that one day she would produce. She was so bad-tempered that she would not allow anyone near the coop on the veranda which I had made for her with bits of tin, sheeting and wire mesh. That, I decided, was the ideal spot. When everyone was fast asleep, I concealed the transmitter under the straw. Henny Penny settled down as if determined to produce a whole family of radios.

I did not even mention the existence of the radio to Dad; it was a secret only Henny Penny and I shared. But Captain Ward's painstaking tuition in his hide-out near the reservoir proved to have been a waste of time. I only found an opportunity to use the set once, and even on that occasion I did not know if the information got through. I doubt it very much. What I had to report was anyway not of such importance that the Allied war effort would have been gravely impaired by its loss.

Although we were deprived of hard news in the camp, rumours were rife that the war would soon be over. We had no way of checking these but hoped desperately that they were true. Certainly, the rumours did not tally with what snippets of information the Japanese gave us, but things were happening which seemed to give us some reasonable grounds for optimism. Japanese morale seemed to be crumbling.

Then strange little incidents began to convince me the war really was approaching its end. Wounded and sick soldiers returning to Maymyo from the battle line began to confide in the railway workers that they had no heart for the war; they even claimed that they had never wanted to fight against the Burmese, they had only done so because the Emperor had decreed it, and no one could disobey him. Some soldiers, returning to the front, borrowed religious medallions to protect them in action, and on their return to Maymyo gratefully returned them, vowing they owed their life to their protective qualities.

Another indication that all was not going well for the Japanese was a surprise visit from Kodama San, who told me he was leaving for the front. The enlistment of a non-combatant like him was evidence that they must be hard pressed, and needed the services of every man capable of firing a rifle. He told me he would do his utmost to keep in touch, but that if he was unable to, he would certainly track me down after the war.

I promised to do the same. We did not say farewell, but lightheartedly agreed that if only one of us survived, he or she would visit the other's country. Kodama was anxious to impress upon me that the *real* Japanese were far removed from the brutal unfeeling soldiers I had encountered in Burma. In his case, I needed no convincing, and I assured him that there was no hatred in my heart for his people.

Then, amidst all the uncertainty, I was given definite news that the end was not far off. During my rounds of a nearby village I made a point of stopping by a banyan tree, where an old man was to be seen squatting with a small pile of vegetables and fruit at his feet, which he would sell or barter. I was trying to exchange something for a few potatoes and some onions, when a voice murmured, 'Follow me.'

I looked round and saw a scruffy old Gurkha, his rags covered with mud and cow dung, his hair matted and filthy. I was so surprised I followed him without question. Only when we were out of earshot of everyone did he ask, 'Remember me? Ernie Devalarez.'

I was so shocked I felt as if I had been pole-axed. I could not believe that the scruffy peasant standing before me was the man who had been gym master at the Shan Chiefs' School in Taunggyi. He told me that when the Japanese invaded he had managed to escape to India and join the paratroops, and that recently he had been dropped back into Burma to establish contact with the underground groups.

'We have heard you are doing a wonderful job, Helen. I have some medicine and some sovereigns and British rupees for you.'

'I'll take the medicine, Ernie, but not the gold or money. As soon as I tried to change any of it I would have to explain where I got it from. The police would immediately suspect I had been in contact with the British.'

Meeting Ernie like that lifted an immense burden from my shoulders, for I was able to tell him about Captain Ward and to pass on the names I had picked up during my interrogation, along with some other information about troop movements.

I met him once more at the same spot, passed on more information, and explained the problem of the transmitter. Ernie said he would shortly be leaving, presumably to rejoin his unit, and I asked him to tell the military authorities where our camp was situated and to make sure orders were given for it not to be bombed. 'That's our greatest fear at the moment. It would be the last straw to have survived this long, only to be killed by our own side at the very end.'

Ernie smiled, and promised to pass on my message.

One unfortunate feature of the approaching climax was that everyone in the camp became very touchy and scared of their own shadow. The uncertainty was communicated to the Japanese, who began to take what seemed to us an exaggerated interest in the problems of security. The formal, somewhat relaxed inspections to which we had become used were replaced by raids on the camp, that might take place at any hour of the day or night. For most of the inhabitants of the camp this was no worse than a slightly alarming inconvenience; for me, knowing what lay hidden below Henny Penny, it was the cause of acute terror. I cursed the moment of weakness in which I had allowed Captain Ward and Bahadur to talk me into sheltering the radio set.

The Japanese were now making frequent arrests, even among those sections of the population that had previously been inviolate. They seemed to have lost their nerve and it was hard to see on what grounds some of their victims could have been selected. I heard that some of those detained had been found in possession of British currency, and I guessed they must have been foolish enough to accept it from British contacts. As the vigilance of the Japanese increased, I became convinced that I was being watched. I was not alone in being ultra-cautious; nearly everyone in the camp began to look over their shoulders and become wary over whom they talked to. People, who had been friends for months or even years, began to suspect each other of being collaborators. I think, in part, that for the first time we were daring to tell ourselves that we

[158]

were likely to survive – and we were determined not to lose out at the last moment. And so we over-reacted and became exaggeratedly prudent and suspicious.

There were two known Japanese sympathisers in the camp; both, I am ashamed to confess, British. We had no direct evidence, of course, but we did not need it. Over the years, we had learned to sniff out sympathisers as easily as a gun dog finds a fallen bird. The signs were self-evident; they had too much money, were never molested by their captors, were often seen indulging in whispered conversations with the guards. We were, of course, all collaborators to a certain extent, insofar as we were polite to the enemy and obeyed his orders, but it was done tongue in cheek, with our own interests uppermost in our minds. We used them unscrupulously to improve our lot, which was vastly different to actively supporting them.

I knew that one of the suspected men had his eye on me and was watching for the first false step I might make. I had no proof, not even enough to entitle me to take action in accordance with our own rough-and-ready code of justice, but I knew I was not indulging in flights of fancy. He was a bitter, disillusioned man who had once worked on the railway; his wife had left him, and his sole interest now was in his personal safety and feathering his own nest. I had noticed that, whereas the majority of the prisoners were concerned with the welfare of their fellow captives, he never lifted a finger to help anyone; in fact, he seldom missed an opportunity to exploit them. He was able to go out of the camp when and how he pleased, and he always had unlimited cash. When food was scarce, he invariably ate well. His favourite method of extortion was to buy food and then sell or barter it, at outrageous prices, to those who were too sick to leave the camp. To my mind, there was only one possible source for his funds: he was an informant.

As more and more people were arrested and given severe beatings to make them talk, my suspicions grew. Among my own informants were Joe and Elias Daniels, sons of the railway family I knew so well. They told me that they were working round the clock, moving Japanese units back and forth to Mandalay. They advised me to be extra careful as the enemy was becoming very jittery; but they were convinced that the Japanese would fight to the bitter end, and deal ruthlessly with anyone who co-operated with the Allies.

Soon after this friendly warning, a squad of soldiers descended on the camp late one night. They burst into the huts and ordered everyone to stand with their hands above their heads while a systematic search was made of their property. They were soldiers I had not seen before, evidently a unit especially ordered in for the raid. I immediately suspected they had been tipped off about something. This was confirmed when the officer said: 'We are looking for a hidden radio.'

There may have been other radios in the camp, but if so I did not know of them. I wondered who could have told them of mine, because I had not mentioned its existence to anyone, not even Dad. What puzzled me even more was that, although the informant evidently knew about the transmitter, it seemed that he could not have known where I had concealed it.

The soldiers went through the block like a swarm of locusts. They lifted the floor, searched under the roof beams, emptied cupboards and ransacked personal belongings. The children were crying, and the older people shaking with fear as, hands above their heads, they were subjected to a none too gentle body search. I can hardly imagine the Japanese expected to find a radio concealed about their persons; perhaps they hoped to find more British currency or other proof of involvement with the enemy.

Henny Penny was clucking like mad, and I thought to myself: 'This is it. She's doing her damnedest to attract attention!' A soldier, who must have read my thoughts, went over to the cage and poked his bayonet through the wire mesh. The bird rose, screeching and squawking, her wings flapping angrily, and pecked furiously at the steel blade. The soldier backed away, grinned toothily, and turned his attention to my personal belongings which he tipped into a heap on the floor.

Then he rummaged through them as if he had been a bargain hunter at a jumble sale.

Mr Nicholas looked at me, and said, 'You look sick, Helen. You must have been overdoing it.' I dared not tell him why I was shaking and sweating.

It was early morning before the search was called off and the soldiers departed, and all that time the prisoners had had to stand with their hands held aloft. By now many of the old people were hysterical; they fell on their knees and began to pray. It took some hours to console the children and get them off to sleep.

In the morning, the man I suspected of being an informer sidled up to me and said: 'Rodriguez, I'm reporting you to the police. You are cutting the ground from under the feet of the Japanese.'

'I have not done anything to justify that allegation,' I retorted angrily. 'Everything I have done has been in the interests of the camp.'

'That's what you say,' he sneered. 'I happen to know different. When I've reported you, the Japanese will find out for themselves.'

I was not going to allow that to happen; memories of Mandalay were still fresh in my mind, and I knew what methods they would adopt to make me talk. I had survived *that* ordeal because I had nothing to hide and so could not tell them anything, but I was not at all confident that, if I was subjected to fresh torture, I would not weaken and betray Henny Penny's secret.

I called one of the younger and fitter men into my cubicle and said: 'Leslie, see to it that that man cannot walk. When he goes for his evening stroll, I want you to attend to him. Get him to the ground and injure his knees. Do the job thoroughly; if he can crawl to the Japs, he will!'

I sat on the edge of my bunk until Leslie poked his head round the corner and gave a thumbs-up sign. Then I knew he had done his duty.

[161]

Soon afterwards, the informer's sister burst in and said: 'Come quickly, please, Helen. My brother's hurt himself. He's in terrible pain. He needs morphia.'

She and her brother knew that I had a little hoard of the pain-killer, because I had on several occasions given some to their mother who was in the terminal stages of cancer. The old lady was the only person I gave it to; it was that precious.

'There is none for your brother. He can suffer! But I will come across and see him.'

Leslie had done a first class job, the wretched man was lying on his bed writhing in agony. I did not feel a flicker of compassion, indeed I admit that I even enjoyed witnessing his pain.

'Someone attacked me in the dark. He tripped me up and injured my knees. I couldn't see who it was. I need morphia,' he begged.

'I have a little aspirin you can have,' I replied.

He groaned, and pleaded with me: 'No, I must have morphia. The pain is unbearable. Please, Helen, just a little.'

'I'm sorry, it is reserved for somebody you know very well.'

His voice assumed a wheedling tone, 'Please, Helen. Please.'

I was totally unmoved. 'So you were going to the Kempetai, were you? That won't be possible now. Is there any message I can deliver for you?'

I looked at him, but he would not return my gaze; instead he lowered his head and began to rub his knees.

'You are a disgrace to your nation,' I said, and walked out.

Some time afterwards, Mr Nicholas called to see me and said that the informer had complained of being attacked in the dark. As headman it was his duty to investigate all complaints. Did I know anything about it? I professed complete ignorance, and he smiled. I knew I was safe for a few more days.

'I will tell him I have made a thorough investigation and have come to the conclusion it was an accident. There is no evidence at all that he was assaulted.'

The man did report me later, but by then it was too late for the Japanese to care; they had enough problems on their hands without bothering about an attack on a man who had outlived his usefulness or whether or not an unimportant nurse was guilty of making contact with the Allies. When the boot was on the other foot, and *I* reported *him* to General Slim's staff, I was lucky enough to get a far better response. He spent some considerable time behind bars.

It was around this time that a Japanese soldier arrived at the camp with a piece of paper with my name written on it. He showed it to me, and when I admitted that I was Helen Rodriguez, he signalled for me to follow him. I asked him where to, for with the situation as precarious as it was it would have been extremely foolhardy to go off with a strange soldier. For all I knew he could be leading me into all kinds of danger.

'I am not going anywhere until you tell me why.'

He would not elaborate beyond saying: 'You will not come to any harm. There is news of a friend.'

I still hesitated, and was extremely reluctant to follow him, but I felt he seemed trustworthy and in the end my curiosity overcame my caution. We walked to the furthest end of the town, where he took me into a bungalow in the heart of the military sector. There I was greeted by a Japanese army doctor who, in a kindly voice, told me to sit down. As he poured tea he explained in broken English that he had been at college with Kodama San, and they were close friends.

'He has written asking me to see you, and offer any help I can. He will not be returning for some time, but he will try to pass on any news through me.'

I thanked him, and said I would be very grateful for any news of Kodama San; at the same time I asked him if he had any medicine to spare. He apologised and said that medical supplies were scarce and badly needed to treat Japanese sick and wounded. He would, however, give me some cotton wool and bottles of disinfectant, and, he added, he would send the messenger for me when he next heard from his friend.

'Please pass on to Kodama San my fondest wishes and say I

pray for his safety,' I said. He solemnly promised to do so, and the messenger escorted me back to the camp.

A long time elapsed before the messenger appeared again and said the doctor wanted to see me. As soon as I entered the bungalow I knew he had bad news, for he was very grave and formal and he bowed before asking me to sit down. 'I am sad to tell you, Kodama Sam has been killed.'

Although I was anticipating bad news, I was shocked when I heard it. I had grown to respect Kodama San and look on him as a true friend, for he had risked his life on numerous occasions to help Dad and me.

'May his soul rest in peace,' I said. I walked slowly and sadly back to the camp, thinking all the time of our pledge to each other when last we had met. I would honour my promise, I vowed, and visit Japan one day.

As the British got closer the air raids intensified. There were two planes I nicknamed Amos and Andy, which came over as regular as clockwork every evening to bomb the railway yards. To do so they had to swoop low over the camp, so that the pilots were clearly visible in their cockpits. As soon as they appeared the cry would go out, '*Hikoki*' (planes). On one occasion, as I watched them drop their bombs, I saw a heavy locomotive hurled like a feather into the air and land upside down on one of the sheds. Next morning I went over to inspect the damage; there were water-filled craters, as big as ponds and the ground was littered with unexploded bombs. The sight increased my nagging fear that the dare-devil fliers would put paid to us before the army arrived. I prayed that Ernie Devalarez had passed on my message but did not feel too certain that, even if he had, it would have got through to the men who actually dropped the bombs.

Soon afterwards Captain Murano summoned Mr Nicholas, myself, and one or two other prisoners to his office. He bowed stiffly and then thanked us for the manner in which we had run the camp. 'Of all the camps I have seen, this is the best,' he said. Then he turned to me, bowed again, and said, '*Kanggofusan*

(Nurse), you have cared for your people admirably. There have been few deaths, and it is the only camp which has kept free of serious contagious diseases. I thank you for keeping them so well and happy. The laughter from your children has lifted my sad heart in this camp. You are young, but you have real courage. Now I must take my leave and bid you goodbye.'

Compliments from an enemy are perhaps not to be sought after, yet I confess that Captain Murano's words gave me nothing but pleasure. George and I thanked him for his fairness and kindness, and for ensuring there were no favourites and that there should be only one rule for everybody.

'You will be happy when your own people are back,' went on Captain Murano. 'We shall remain here and fight to the death. Soon I shall take the sentries from the gate. I will need every man for combat duties.'

I begged him not to do that. 'If you remove the sentries you might as well ask us to commit suicide. The Burmese will rush in and slaughter us for the little food and property we have.'

'I cannot guarantee how my men will behave, but I will do my best to protect you. In the meantime, you must bring in your fences so as to make the compound smaller and easier to defend.'

As he saluted and turned to walk away I burst into tears. 'This is going to be the worst period we have lived through,' I said to George Nicholas. 'We must not crack now. The British cannot be far off.'

When the sentries were withdrawn, I got a few of the young and more able-bodied men and women to lift out the posts and bring in the wire fences until the compound was much smaller. I recalled how I had seen hillmen fashion primitive weapons out of bamboo, and I got everyone capable of wielding an axe or machete to cut as many canes as possible. The ends were sharpened, then roasted in the fire, until the tips were as hard as flint and lethal as spears. Mr Nicholas and I then drew up a round-the-clock sentry roster; no one except the most elderly was excused, women and children all had to take their turn.

[165]

Mercifully our precautions were unnecessary. Perhaps I over-estimated the aggressive nature of the Burmese, or perhaps they were deterred by our obvious readiness to defend ourselves.

Many dates elude me, but 11th March, 1945, is emblazoned in my memory like a fiery cross. It was the day the British re-occupied Maymyo.

I was on sentry duty with Jessie Lafranais and just as dawn was breaking I heard the unusual sound of horses whinnying and the rumble of cart wheels. Jessie helped me to clamber on to the roof of the washhouse, and from there an amazing sight greeted my eyes. Lumbering towards the camp, throwing up great clouds of dust, was a column of bullock-drawn carts, with Gurkha soldiers marching steadily alongside. The white tops of the wagons were billowing in the wind, reminding me of an old Wild West wagon train. I shouted excitedly to Jessie, and hauled her up beside me. As the convoy got nearer, I realised the flapping white tops were parachutes which the Gurkhas were using to hold down their equipment. Leading the long, winding column were two British officers on beautifully groomed horses.

One of these then held his arm up and roared out an order, and seconds later the Gurkhas started setting up their guns and digging themselves in. To my horror I realised that they were aiming their gun-sights at the camp. I jumped down and screamed for Jessie to follow me. We ran as fast as our legs would carry us, tripping over stones and bumping into boulders, but we ignored the cuts and bruises and just kept on running. I was shouting all the time: 'For God's sake, don't shoot. It's us. It's us.'

I ran up to a captain on one of the horses, and said breath-lessly: 'Sir, *we* are in that camp. We are internees. There are four hundred of us. Please tell your men not to fire.'

He leaned down, picked me up with one arm and swung me on to his horse. 'Who are you, and where are you from?'

I explained that I had been on sentry duty when I spotted the column, and had rushed out of the camp to prevent it being shelled. 'We have been here nineteen months, living for this day, and we don't want to die now.'

He patted me on the shoulder, smiled and said: 'Don't worry, that won't happen.'

The Japanese had concentrated in the railway yard, and without warning their guns now opened fire. They had not quite got the range, even so the first shells fell far too close for comfort. The officer lifted me off his horse and bellowed out an order. The next thing I knew, Jessie and I were in a slit trench, listening to the scream and whistle of the shells and the explosions which resembled continuous thunder. The barrage stopped as abruptly as it had started, and the silence was awesome. I poked my head over the top of the trench and saw a grinning Gurkha looking at me. 'Breakfast, memsahib,' he said.

Jessie and I scrambled out, and our nostrils were greeted with a variety of smells we never thought we would experience again: fried eggs, bacon, freshly baked bread, beans, and brewing tea and coffee. Heaven knows how such plentiful supplies had reached the front line – we did not waste time enquiring.

We were taken to a mess tent where plates, heaped with food, were placed in front of us. At nights I had often dreamed of such a feast, followed by hot toast and marmalade, yet when the dream came true, I had to push it away. I just could not eat. But I enjoyed my first cup of coffee for two years.

I said to the captain, 'If you don't mind, sir, I would like to return to the camp; they will be worried sick wondering what has happened to us.'

The captain and a small escort took us back to the camp, where Mr Nicholas and a handful of friends were waiting anxiously at the gate.

'But for these two young ladies you would all be dead,' said the captain. 'Somebody told us this was a Japanese strong-point, and we were going to blow it out of existence.'

Later that day, a bullock cart arrived, piled high with food, cigarettes and even some bottles of whisky.

The fight for Maymyo was short but very bitter. The relieving brigade had broken away from the main force heading for Mandalay, and struck north-east. They had marched non-stop for four days along little-known tracks used by opium smugglers, over two ranges of mountains, then through the beautiful valley leading to the town. The Japanese garrison was caught unawares. Some managed to flee in a train that happened to be in the station, but the majority were wiped out among the houses and bungalows and flower-lined streets. An enemy convoy was ambushed, and forty lorries were captured, which temporarily solved the transport problem.

It took some time for us to realise that the moment we had lived and prayed for had at last arrived, but when the truth did dawn we became delirious with joy. The women wept, flung their arms around the soldiers and showered them with kisses, while the men pumped their hands as if they were intent on shaking them off. The same three words were shouted by everyone, 'We are free. We are free.'

I went into my cubicle and knelt and prayed. It was so hard to believe it was true.

Chapter 9

One morning soon after the arrival of the British, I was sitting by my bunk when I heard the rattle of machine guns and the roar of aircraft passing overhead. It had been easy to delude oneself that everything was now done, the fighting finished. These sounds from what I had fondly imagined to be the past rudely reminded me that, although I was free, the war was not yet over. The machine gun fire came from troops mopping up those few Japanese who remained in the vicinity and were prepared to die rather than surrender. The planes were our own, straffing the few remaining enemy strongholds.

I could hear the crump of exploding bombs in the distance, and shuddered at the thought of what the Japanese were going through. It was not until an almost demented Indian ran into the camp, appealing for volunteers to help the wounded, that I learned there had been a ghastly mistake. The planes had bombed a refugee settlement about six or seven miles away on the north side of the town. I say 'mistake' because the Indian assumed they were British planes; no one in the settlement had been able to identify them and it is conceivable that in this case they were Japanese, launching a final and desperate attack.

I packed all the medicine I had and set off with several other volunteers to walk to the settlement. The British were far too busy tackling the enemy to be approached for transport. I needed no signpost, for as I set off a pall of black smoke was rising slowly into the air, darkening the distant skyline.

I had heard vague rumours about the refugee settlement, but had not had cause to go there before. It turned out to be a mixed community of the better-off Hindus, Mohammedans, Chinese and Burmese, who had shelved their religious and cultural differences and set up a small farming community.

All I could hear as I walked into the devastated village was one long mournful groan, which seemed to be coming out of the earth itself. I realised that many people were trapped below the smouldering debris of their homes. People were scrabbling with their bare hands in an attempt to tear away the burning timber and rescue the emtombed victims. The air reeked with the sickening smell of charred flesh, and the dusty roads were littered with dead horses, cows, dogs, cats and humans.

One of the distraught villagers told me that they had all built air raid shelters under the floor which could be entered by a trap door. This meant that they did not have to leave the house when enemy planes approached, but when the bombs fell and roofs and walls collapsed, the people in the shelters were left with no way of escaping.

As the rescue work went on, I told those who had escaped injury or were not too badly burned to collect as much cloth as they could lay their hands on – anything would do – dhotis, saris, sheets – and every drop of oil in the village. It did not matter if it was cooking oil or castor oil.

I got huge fires burning so as to boil large cauldrons of water and oil. As the cloth was brought to me, I dropped it into the boiling oil, and told those attending the fires to take it out after a few minutes and let it cool.

As the trapped people were brought to safety they were laid out in a long line on the ground. Several years of nursing amid the horrors of war had taught me to shut off my mind to all distractions beyond the work in hand, but hardened as I was I found it impossible to rise above the chorus of screams and groans which seemed to fill the entire settlement. I started with the children. I had never seen burns as bad before, and it took a considerable effort not to be violently sick. The skin was hanging from their arms, legs, chests and faces, like peeled wallpaper. The skin on the soles of the feet and the palms of the hands is always the toughest and thickest, but in many cases even this had been burned down to the bone. I snipped off the charred flesh as best I could with a pair of scissors, and let the pieces fall into a bucket. When I had finished this gory task, the people helped me to roll the oil bandages over the terrible injuries. Some of the victims were burned so badly that by the time we had finished they resembled Egyptian mummies, literally swathed from head to foot. People were passing out all around me, and I got someone to make up a weak mixture of rum and water with which to revive them.

I worked on, bent double, until I felt like dropping from exhaustion. After the children, I started on the women; finally I turned to the men.

Horses were whinnying in pain, and badly injured domestic pets were crawling through the dust, writhing in agony. There was nothing I could do for them, and so I ordered the villagers to put them out of their misery.

Many of the entombed people were dead when they were brought out, and I gave orders for huge pits to be dug as communal graves. The Mohammedans were buried separately from the others, although it was not always possible to identify the bodies; they were horribly mutilated and disfigured, just chunks of blackened flesh.

When it was too dark to work any longer, the headman provided a cart to take me and the other volunteers back to the camp. He pleaded with me to return next morning, but I said I could not walk so far again; if they required assistance, he would have to send transport.

On the journey back, the cries of those unfortunate people still rang in my ears. They had endured so much, and had only managed to survive because they were strengthened by the hope that one day it would finish. Now, when it had seemed their troubles were almost over, it had indeed ended for them – but how cruel an end it proved to be.

At first light a horse-drawn gharry arrived to take me and a handful of helpers out to the settlement. When I got there, the fires were already burning, and the pots of oil and water boiling on them. Having seen how exhausting it had been for me to work in the blazing sun, the villagers had erected a small bamboo structure with a thatched roof to keep the heat off my back. Still more thoughtfully, they had provided a long trestle table so that I would not have to bend to treat the injured.

I worked methodically throughout the morning, concentrating one hundred per cent on my task. What can have happened to disturb that concentration I cannot even surmise, but suddenly I felt a thrill of alarm and some inner instinct made me throw myself on the ground. As I did so, a bullet whistled over my head. Pandemonium broke out as the villagers began to chase the man who had fired a rifle at me. When they caught him and dragged him in front of me, the headman said he was a total stranger who came from a different area. When I asked him why he had tried to kill me, he said he would kill anyone who helped the wounded. Beyond that he would not say a word. The experience so unnerved me that I could not stop shaking; but there was no time to indulge in such weakness for long. Soon I was back at work again and when the wretched man was dragged off into the jungle to be dealt with, I did not give a second thought to the fate that awaited him.

When news of the disaster reached the army, lorries were rushed to the village to take the wounded to the military hospital which had been set up in Maymyo. I could not help reflecting what a tragic irony it was. Those poor souls had waited for two years for the British to return, and this was how their unswerving loyalty had been rewarded. The deep bitterness it aroused among the victims was understandable.

It took the British several days to mop up the remaining Japanese, then they got around to us. The first step was to take down all our particulars, and the names and addresses of any next of kin who it was believed had managed to reach India.

While this was going on, George Nicholas and I decided to conduct a final tour of the camp so as to make sure that no one had been overlooked. We became aware of an awful smell coming from just outside our original perimeter. When we went to investigate we almost stumbled over the decomposed body of Captain Murano who had shot himself through the head. He had been lying there for some time. We decided to give him a decent burial in the Christian cemetery. It was the least we could do, we felt, for he had been a fair man, who had done what he could to help us and grant our requests, especially where the young or the elderly were concerned. As we lifted his body on to a makeshift stretcher, we met a party of British soldiers who were coming into the camp so as to invite thirty or forty of the younger women to a dance that evening. An officer stared disbelievingly at the tears streaming down my cheeks, and said angrily: 'So this is what we've been fighting for! We kill them so that you can weep over them.'

I was so outraged that I took off one of my home-made wooden shoes and struck him in the face. He stiffened, then turned and walked away. I felt sick at heart. I should have tried to curb my foul temper. What else could one expect an officer to say when confronted by such a scene? He had seen his men killed, and the Japanese had shed no tears for them. How could he be expected to understand that we might feel grief over the death of an honourable man, even if he had been one of the enemy?

George Nicholas put his arm around me, and said: 'You were not to blame, Helen. Just forget about it.' The disagreeable incident shook us badly but did not deter us from burying Captain Murano in the local cemetery.

As the days passed we slowly began to adapt to our new way of life. Our rations were first class, and there was plenty of cigarettes and liquor. Even Dad showed signs of chirping up, with lots to read and a nightly tot of whisky, while for the younger women there were plenty of dances, with good-looking young soldiers.

I had done as Mr Nicholas advised, and completely erased from my mind the incident of Captain Murano's funeral and the British officer. Unfortunately, the officer had not. My blow had cost him a tooth, and thus injured both his pride and his feelings. He had reported me officially, and I was soon requested to call on one of General Slim's staff. The staff officer looked at me sternly, and said: 'I have had some excellent reports about you, Miss Rodriguez. Then you have to spoil it all by striking an officer. What am I going to do with you?'

'You can do what the hell you like,' I snapped, 'but let me tell you this. No Japanese ever touched a woman here, and that was due to Captain Murano, the man we were burying when your officer came along. We had to wait until the British arrived before anyone lost their virginity!'

He nodded, and told me I could go; he would have to give the matter some thought, he said.

Soon afterwards a formal banquet was held with the army as host. I was invited to be guest of honour, but I did not think I deserved the tribute and said I thought it should go to an older woman. In the end I compromised and shared the honour with another woman from the camp. One reason for my reluctance was that I did not have a decent dress to wear, but a soldier helped me overcome the problem by presenting me with a yellow silk parachute. This I made into a very presentable ball gown. The reception was held in a beautiful house which we called Number 10 Downing Street and which had once belonged to a wealthy forestry officer.

There were toasts and speeches, and the tables were laden with the most gorgeous food. My best moment came when I danced with General Slim. I wondered whether he had heard anything about my assault on his staff officer. I soon found out that he had. 'I hear you are a bit of a spitfire,' he remarked, but his eyes were twinkling.

Next morning I was rather vague in my recollections of the occasion; I had drunk far more than was good for me. After such a long period of enforced abstinence I did not have much of a head for strong drink. But of one thing I felt sure; the incident of the shoe would never be raised again.

A bad bout of cholera now put me out of action for several

weeks, but when I recovered I realised that I had to do something about Dad, and do it quickly. The brief uplift in his spirits after our liberation had soon passed. If I did not get him to India he would die. It was only the thought of being reunited with Mother that had kept him going so long. There were others too who would not survive if they did not receive prompt hospital treatment. And so I pestered the army for seats to be made available for the sick and aged aboard the aircraft which were flying regularly to India. Always I found myself being strangled by red tape. I threatened, swore, threw tantrums, begged and cajoled, but all fell on deaf ears. The colonel who was allegedly in charge of repatriation just wasn't interested in my father and others like him, although aircraft which flew in supplies often flew out empty. He was never short of excuses or explanations, but none of them seemed to me to have any real force. Weeks passed, and he still would not budge. What annoyed me most was that military personnel and, indeed, some civilians, had already been flown to India for medical treatment. I discovered this when Captain Ward called and thanked me for my help. He looked pale and ill, and said he was being sent to a hospital in India. If anyone deserved it he did, but there were others who had suffered as much. I could not see why they were being ignored when the facilities to help them were available.

In the end I decided to try to make my own arrangements. I discovered that people were being flown out from Meiktila airstrip and it occurred to me that my problems might be solved if only I could get there. I made enquiries, and was told three seats would be made available on a plane from there, but that I would have to make my own arrangements to get to the airstrip. Fortunately, I had become friendly with a young captain in charge of a transport unit, and I persuaded him to let me have the use of a 15-cwt. truck and driver. I knew that he was taking a risk and was liable to end up on a charge, but he was acutely aware of Dad's conditions, and he did not hesitate to come to the rescue.

Next morning, I shaved Dad, sponged him down, and dressed him in clean clothes. He looked awful, and I knew in my heart that this would be goodbye; I would never see him again. I also found space on the truck for Mr Nicholas and Mr Gibbs. I had been told that one of the three seats was for me, but I preferred to give it to somebody else as I felt I could not fly out leaving my family to fend for themselves.

The day before we were due to leave, an old friend flew in from India, called me aside and said: 'Helen, I have some sad news. Your mother is dead.'

I did not know what to say or do. I could not tell Dad, for the news would kill him, and so I went on with all the arrangements as though they were going to culminate in a happy reunion.

On 2nd June, we drove to Meiktila, although the Japanese were still in the area and putting up stiff resistance. We arrived in the middle of an air raid, but the transport pilots did not let that stop them and I saw Dad, Mr Nicholas and Mr Gibbs safely aboard. I stood on the tarmac until the aircraft was a distant speck in the sky, then climbed into the truck and returned to Maymyo. I wrote in my diary: 'Heartbreaking to say goodbye to Dad. I don't think I shall see him again.'

It was not until fifteen days later that I had a long telex message from Mr Nicholas telling me that all my labours had been in vain. Dad had died in the Presidency General Hospital, Calcutta, two days after arriving in India. The good news was that my friend had misinformed me. Mother was alive and well, although she had not been able to reach Dad in time; in fact, she had even been too late for the funeral. My only consolation was that Mr Nicholas had been at his bedside so Dad had not died alone and friendless.

I made up my mind that I could not stay in Maymyo; as soon as I had got the children settled in new homes I would clear out. I managed to trace a relative of Rosalind's who arranged for an aircraft to fly her to a forward airstrip on the Mandalay front, where they were reunited. The Pugh girls also joined up with some relatives, while the nuns agreed to look after the King children until something permanent could be arranged.

I hated parting from them, I had grown to love them all so much, but I knew their future could not be with me. In any case, I accepted that at some time in the not too distant future, I would have to go to India to find Mother.

Before handing over the children, I took them to All Saints Church where a service of thanksgiving was being held. All the beautiful stained glass windows were smashed and the lovely altar desecrated, but it was still God's house, and as I knelt to pray I felt a deep inner peace flowing through me. I sang Gounod's 'Ave Maria' as a solo, and when we emerged into the sunlight one of the children, disturbed at my silence, said: 'Aunt Helen, say something.'

I embraced them one by one and asked: 'What is there to say? I love you all.'

We parted with tears streaming down our cheeks. At least I had one thing to be grateful to the Japanese for.

I felt lost and alone and very sorry for myself, but my spirits soared soon afterwards when an envelope came through the letter box:

'Dearest Aunt Helen,
    Words cannot express how much my heart is filled with gratitude for all you have done for me. At times I was a real nuisance, but for your kind heart you did forgive me every time. I have still fresh in my memory the good deed you did for my sister Doris, and my dad. Maybe then I did not realise what it really meant, but now when you have to leave us I realise carefully all you have done for the children of J. A. King. God alone knows what would have happened to me and the two little ones if we were left alone. Now, Aunt Helen dear, please try and always remember me as a good girl, forgive all the other deeds of my faults and when I grow older I will try to come to the height you have reached. God will bless you wherever you go, and will reward

[177]

you in the highest. Goodbye Aunt Helen and I will always remember you as my own m-o-t-h-e-r.

Love from the two little ones, Richard and Maria, and the rest from Snookums.'

I make no apology for printing the letter in its entirety; they were my children and always will be. That parting letter is my most prized possession. It has travelled with me wherever I have been, and over the years it has brought me immense comfort.

Chapter 10

The peace I had found in prayer at All Saints quickly deserted me, and the bitterness over the way Dad had been treated returned, no doubt because I was so terribly depressed at parting with my children. I needed to immerse myself in work, otherwise I would wallow in a quagmire of self-pity. So I made what few arrangements were necessary, said farewell to those who had suffered so long and so cheerfully and then set off for Mandalay to work in the nearby leper colony.

The nuns there had made my own contribution to the war effort seem pitiful indeed. Throughout the occupation they had cared for and treated over a hundred people. Not all of these were lepers, for some had sought sanctuary there knowing that it was a safe haven from the Japanese who were terrified of the poor, disfigured souls who had lost fingers, arms, legs, ears and noses.

The nuns, despite their deep sense of vocation, had been extremely practical during the occupation, and knowing the obsessive fear that the Japanese felt for any contagious disease, had deliberately capitalised on it. Mother Oliver confided to me that, whenever a military convoy passed by, she had sent out the lepers to chase the vehicles, screaming to the soldiers that they would scratch them if they did not provide food. The Japanese in their terror would toss food over the tailboards before roaring off at full speed. In this way, Mother Oliver and her group of nursing nuns had kept the little community alive.

The night I arrived, I said to her: 'I want you to remove this bitterness from my heart. I cannot go through life consumed with resentment because I feel my father was badly treated.'

She looked at me with great compassion, and said: 'My darling, there is nothing I can do for you. It is something between you and your Maker. You are a young woman who has been through too much in too short a time, whereas I am an old lady who has lived a lifetime, and discovered that forgiveness is the greatest healer. You must learn that too. Just stay here as long as you feel you can. You are welcome.'

I pondered on her words, but at first could not find the strength to forgive. I went to the chapel and waited outside until the nuns had completed their evening prayers, then I went inside. I did not kneel but simply sat staring into space. It was a bare, white-walled room with one small crucifix on the wall. As I sat there, I seemed to hear an inner voice and peace returned to my heart. I could feel the help flooding through me, giving me strength to carry on. I do not know how long I sat there, but in the end a nun was sent to fetch me. She put her arms around me and led me to a room where some food had been laid out.

I am not a good Catholic, I'm not even a good Christian, but I have never lost my faith. Despite all that I have witnessed and suffered, I can still say: 'There is a God.' I have faith and hope, and know that Christ never gives us a cross heavier than we can bear.

I stayed among the lepers until I had worked myself back into a state of contentment, then I made plans to go to Calcutta. I flew from Meiktila and, as soon as I had landed, went to the hospital where Dad had died to find out where he was buried. I tracked down his grave in the cemetery, unmarked by any stone, just by a name and number plate. But the bitterness did not return. Dad was at last at peace.

On 1st July, 1945, I stepped off the train at the Cantonment Station, Bangalore, and there, waiting by the ticket barrier, was my mother. Despite all that she had gone through, she was smiling, and as we embraced the tears that poured un-ashamedly down our cheeks were tears of joy. I put my kitbag on her cycle and said: 'Let's go home, Mum.'

It was some months later when I was working in Hyderabad, that I learned I had been awarded the George Medal for my work in Taunggyi. Apparently, attempts had been made to trace my whereabouts, and when I was finally found I was invited to go to Rangoon to be invested with the medal by the Governor of Burma, Sir Reginald Dorman-Smith. I declined, and asked for the award to be sent to me in the post. I had no intention of meeting Sir Reginald, whom I considered had let us down badly in Burma. He had urged us to stick to our posts, then he himself had flown out in a private plane. I may have been unfair to Sir Reginald, but it was a view shared by many Burma veterans. It is a view I still hold; to my way of thinking, the captain should be last to leave the ship, not first.

The medal was not sent to me as requested, but to the Secunderabad Residency, where Sir Arthur Lothian was approaching the end of his period of office as Resident. Sir Walter Monckton, the distinguished lawyer, was constitutional adviser to the Nizam at the time, and he tried to persuade me to attend the investiture at the Residency. At first I refused. I did not feel that the Government had played fair by the victims of the Japanese invasion and was not prepared to condone their behaviour in any way. Major General 'Boy' Browning then had a go at persuading me, but I was not interested. I knew it was a great honour that was being done me, but I had not done my duty to win a medal; I had stayed because I had a job to do. As for medals, I regarded them as pretty useless things anyway.

Eventually Lord Louis Mountbatten convinced me that I should attend the investiture; he wrote saying that otherwise it would be a slight on Sir Arthur who would shortly be retiring.

The citation, which had appeared in the *London Gazette* on 8th May, 1942, said:

> Miss Hellen Rodriguez, Matron, Civil Hospital, Taunggyi, Burma. When Taunggyi was attacked by two waves of Japanese bombers Miss Rodriguez dis-
> played the utmost courage and devotion to duty. The

military hospital was bombed and in the absence of stretcher bearers, Miss Rodriguez carried patients on her back to places of safety. While performing this heroic task she was bombed and machine-gunned. She returned to the civil hospital and herself performed many operations, remaining on duty with practically no sleep for four days and nights. Her courage and initiative and complete disregard for her own safety were in the highest traditions of the Nursing Service.

Apart from spelling my Christian name wrongly, the account was all too flattering. I was proud and honoured, although I did not know, and still do not know, who recommended me for an award. I can only assumed that it was Colonel Brocklehurst before he died.

The investiture was a sumptuous affair, with everybody dressed to the nines and being waited on hand and foot by bearers in magnificent uniforms, gaily coloured turbans and cummerbunds. It was just like the Raj at its zenith. I wore my uniform for the presentation, but changed later into my parachute dress, brightened with some attractive black lace.

The champagne flowed. Sir Arthur said a few words: 'I am sure we are all proud to have this brave woman with us here today.' There was polite applause, then the festivities began. I had the first dance with Sir Arthur, the next with Sir Walter Monckton, who was extremely flattering about my dress, unaware that not so long ago it had parachuted a soldier into Burma.

Soon afterwards I had an unexpected windfall in the form of a letter from the Government of Burma, Frontier Area Administration and Development Department, Rangoon, which had been forwarded to me by the Accountant General, Burma. It recounted my period in Taunggyi and said:

'She remained behind in this country and attended to the wounded despite strong arguments to evacuate from the Military Commander of Taunggyi and the

Commissioner, Federated Shan States. Though the Matron had to face odds she continued to carry on the good work till the return of the British.'

I started to skip lines, until my eyes caught the next clause, couched in the most tortuous officialese: 'I am to say further that in recognition of her meritorious services, the Governor with the previous sanction of the Secretary of State, sanctions the grant to her of an honorarium of a sum of Rs 5000 – (Rupees five thousand only). Against this sum should be adjusted the sum of Rs 900 – (Rupees nine hundred only) – paid to Miss Rodriguez in 1945 and I am to request that payment of the balance of Rs 4100 – (Rupees four thousand and one hundred only) – be made to her as early as possible.'

I had a good chuckle over the governmental jargon and felt like calling for three cheers for Sir Reginald. The writer may have been anxious to make sure that I did not get a rupee more than I was entitled to, but it was still the best news I had received for years.

And so life began again. After Hyderabad and the coming of independence to India, I worked for a while in Ootacamund and elsewhere in South India. There I helped to set up an experimental ambulance service and worked for a time with that wonderful man, Group Captain Leonard Cheshire. In Bangalore I spent some years with the amazing medical missionary Dr Ida Scudder, and nursed her during her final illness when she was nearly ninety. I also worked with Mother Theresa in the slums of Calcutta. It was a full and happy life, and I hope a useful one.

In 1962 I went with my mother to Japan. This was the fulfilment of the pledge I had made so many years before to my dear friend Kodama San. I visited his home town of Kyoto, the ancient 'capital of peace and tranquillity', and made every effort to trace his brother, who had also been educated at mission schools in Japan and Canada. To my great sorrow I found that he had returned to Vancouver.

[183]

Kyoto is a beautiful city of palaces, shrines, temples and gardens, with a main street as wide as a motorway lined with countless willows. The Allies never bombed it. To me it summed up all that was best and most noble in Japanese art and culture. Kodama San had said that if I ever went to Kyoto, I should visit the pagoda of a thousand Buddhas. He would be there. I knew, of course, that he would not; he had died in Burma. And yet, as I walked along the corridor, lined with hundreds of small, wooden Buddhas, I underwent a strange experience. The little ornaments on the statues tinkled, and there was a slight whispering, like a gentle breeze in a pine forest. Suddenly I felt extremely cold, and I stood absolutely still, although there were many other tourists there at the time. It was then I heard his voice: 'Helen, it is I, Kodama San. Thank you, and God bless you.'

I felt a great warmth flowing through me, and knew he was at peace. At the same time I found peace too. Kyoto for me was a place where I found tranquillity. I did not try to rationalise the experience; it had happened, and I accepted it. People could scoff, as much as they liked; I did not care. Some things happen to which we have no key, some questions will never be answered.

When I got outside I turned to Mother and said: 'Did you hear anything in there?' She looked at me and said: 'Yes, Helen, I did, I heard.'

My friends sometimes seem amazed when I tell them I bear no bitterness towards the Japanese, but I have much to be grateful to them for. There were many good and honourable men among them, notably Kodama San, who befriended my father and me as if we had been members of his own family. But for the Japanese, too, I would never have had the joy of my own 'children', or made so many lifelong friends. In Burma, I witnessed the indestructible courage of humans under adversity, and learned too the importance of humility, service and faith.

Today I am a sick woman, confined to a wheelchair, almost

entirely immobile. But I have my faith to support me. Although I can no longer go to church, I can sit and look out over Hounslow Heath, which is finer than any cathedral, and know that my Maker, from whom I get my strength, is there. I have my birds which give me so much pleasure and ask so little in return. On the sitting room wall are the two plates I salvaged from Craigmore, and by my bed is the plaster statue of the Virgin Mary which Rosalind gave to me in Maymyo, and which never toppled over even in the fiercest air raid.

I still get many letters from the people I got to know during these years, or from their children. Two or three of them did not know my full name and wrote to me as 'Helen of Burma'. That is what Lady Mountbatten called me too – and since her husband was Earl Mountbatten of Burma, she was surely an authority on the subject! Helen of Burma I certainly feel myself, for it was there that I passed some of the happiest and the most painful years of my life.

I am content. I have no wish for material possessions. I do not care if I eat off a gold plate or a plantain leaf. I have always tried to live according to a few simple rules: be truthful, honest, loyal to my Queen, and the Crown, and by that I mean the Crown of Heaven. If I have served others it was not because I sought honours. A George Medal is of little use in a high-rise block of flats. I did what I did because it was my duty. And by doing it, I have found what no riches can purchase. Serenity.

Epilogue

Helen did not complete her book as she would have wished. She was taken seriously ill while recording her final experiences, and died a few hours later. She asked for her ashes to be flown to India and scattered on the hill in Kodaikanal near Solheim, which held so many happy memories. The statue of the Virgin Mary she bequeathed to Rosalind.